A COMPANY OF FORTS

Kidwelly castle.

A Company of Forts

A Guide to the Medieval Castles of west Wales

Paul Davis

First Impression – 1987 (*Published as Castles of Dyfed*)
Revised Edition – 2000

ISBN 1 85902 839 X

Many thanks to Neil Ludlow (Dyfed Archaeological
Trust) for offering suggestions on the development of
Carmarthen and Narberth Castles.

Printed in Wales by
Gomer Press, Llandysul, Ceredigion

Cover illustrations
    Front cover: Laugharne.
    Back cover: Newcastle Emlyn
               Manorbier
               Dinefwr

For T. B. & the 5½ months

'The castles that stand like a company of forts, may not be forgotten, their buyldings are so princely, their strength is so greate, and they are such stately seates and defences of nature.'

Thomas Churchyard 1587.

In the three counties of Ceredigion, Carmarthenshire, and Pembrokeshire there are the remains of around 150 Medieval castles, tower houses and the like. They range from modest overgrown earthworks to massive stone constructions; immaculately kept visitor-friendly ruins, and crumbling fragments swathed in dense undergrowth. All are relics of the time when the countryside of Wales knew little peace from the depredations of invader and defender, and when the ruling elite were forced to protect themselves and their estates by building fortified power bases.

A castle by definition is a Medieval fortification and a by-product of the feudal system, and so hillforts of Iron Age and Roman date (which often carry the prefix 'castle') are not included. The following text is arranged in four sections. First there is an introduction to put the castles in their proper historical perspective; then an architectural survey and guide to the castles of timber (part 2) and stone (part 3); followed by a look at tower houses and peripheral fortifications (part 4). Finally there is a glossary and a list of references.

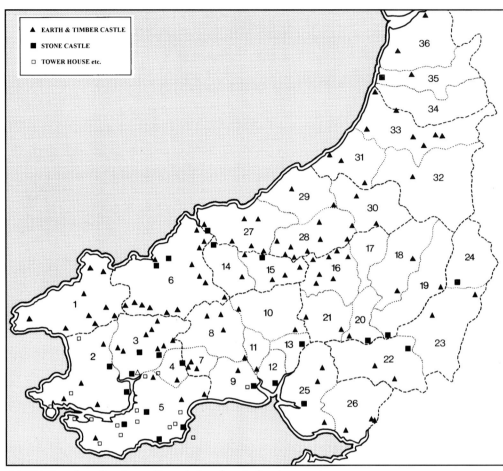

MAP 1. Location of castles and boundaries of *cantrefi* and *commotes*.

1 Pebidiog
2 Rhos
3 Daugleddau
4 Arberth
5 Penfro
6 Cemais
Gwarthaf
7 Efelffre
8 Peuliniog
9 Talacharn
10 Elfed
11 Ystlwyf
12 Penrhyn
13 Derllys
Emlyn
14 Is Cych
15 Uwch Cych

Cantref Mawr
16 Mabudrud
17 Mabelfyw
18 Caio
19 Manordeilo
20 Cethiniog
21 Gwidigada
Cantref Bychan
22 Is Cennen
23 Perfedd
24 Hirfryn
25 Cydweli
26 Carnwyllion

Is Aeron
27 Iscoed
28 Gwynionydd
29 Caerwedros
30 Mabwynion
Uwch Aeron
31 Anhuniog
32 Penardd
33 Mefenydd
Penweddig
34 Creuddyn
35 Perfedd
36 Geneu'r Glyn

HISTORICAL INTRODUCTION

WALES on the eve of the Norman invasion was a land fragmented into small territories and petty kingdoms ruled by minor dynasties from a *llys* (court) in each province. There were three main territorial divisions – Gwynedd, Powys and Deheubarth, with lesser territories including Morgannwg, Gwent and Brycheiniog. We are concerned here with Deheubarth that, at its greatest extent, comprised the whole of south-west Wales. Within the fluctuating boundaries lay twelve territorial divisions called *cantrefi*, which in turn were split into smaller units, *commotes* (see map 1).

One of the main sources of information for this early period is the *Brut y Tywysogion* (Chronicles of the Princes), a yearly journal of events ranging from the seventh century to the early fourteenth century. The Chronicles paint a bleak and violent picture of a land seething with minor kings and ruling families ceaselessly at war with each other, and the catalogue of fighting, raiding, vendettas, and murders can make depressing reading. The scene that emerges is of a situation comparable to modern day Bosnia or the Middle East. There were times when charismatic and ruthless leaders such as Rhodri Mawr (d.878) and Gruffudd ap Llywelyn (d.1063) might succeed in uniting the warring factions under one rule, but the results were always short-lived.

THE NORMANS IN WEST WALES.

The entry in the *Brut y Tywysogion* for the year 1066 has an undisguised, but ill-timed, note of rejoicing in the announcement of King Harold's death in battle. The Saxon king had been harassing the Welsh for some time, but his successor was to pose a far greater threat to native independence. Within a relatively short time Anglo-Saxon England

was brought under Norman rule, and the warlords spread north and west to the borders of Wales in search of more lands to seize. But it was to take more than two centuries before the heartland of Wales was effectively conquered.

By the last quarter of the eleventh century Rhys ap Tewdwr (d.1093) had established himself as ruler of Deheubarth, fending off Norman raiders in 1073 and 1074. In 1081 King William I (1066-87) and his army travelled through south Wales as far as St Davids to make what the *Brut* describes as a 'pilgrimage', but what was in reality a show of strength. Rhys came to terms with the king and was left to rule Deheubarth on payment of a tribute. But with quarrelsome Welsh neighbours and avaricious Normans ensconced on his borders, the end was not far off. In 1093 Rhys was killed in battle near Brecon, and the last obstacle for a full-scale invasion of west Wales was removed.

The unknown chronicler of the *Brut* lamented how *'the French over-ran Dyfed and Ceredigion . . . and made castles in them and fortified them'*. There were two main advances; the sheriff of Devon, William fitz Baldwin (d.1096), sailed up the Tywi estuary and built a castle at Rhydygors (later known as Carmarthen); while Roger de Montgomery (d.1094) marched from his mid-Wales base and established Dingeraint (Cardigan) and Pembroke.

The strategic use of castles was the key to Norman military tactics, and they had been built in western Europe since the ninth century. A fortified base could be established fairly quickly in an invaded territory and would be used as a springboard for further advance. The primary function of a castle was the fortified dwelling of the ruling elite, but it also worked as an administrative centre and, more potently perhaps, the physical and symbolic presence of a foreign power. Conquered territories would be parcelled out among the followers of the chief lord in return for military service during a certain period of the year.

The settlement pattern employed by the Normans was to first establish a military base, then encourage the development of an adjoining settlement at certain key sites. Towns and villages were necessary in bringing some measure of economic stability to an invaded territory. The traditional image of a rural village – church, castle, manor house and dwellings clustered around a green – is an innovation developed by the Anglo-Norman settlers. There is evidence that some castles were founded on, or near, existing settlements, and not all of the Norman urban developments survived to the present day. In the turbulent twelfth century the civilian population was as much at risk from attack as the castle garrison.

Only three castles are specifically mentioned in 1093, but we can assume that more were built by Roger and William's followers. However, the invaders had over-reached themselves, and in the following year the Welsh counterattacked, driving the Normans out of west Wales. Only Pembroke and Rhydygors held out, and when William died in 1096 the garrison abandoned Rhydygors.

The building of Hastings motte castle, drawn from the Bayeux Tapestry.

THE ANGLO-NORMAN CONSOLIDATION.

By the beginning of the twelfth century the political situation in Wales had changed, and an uneasy status quo emerged. Henry I (1100-35) realised the difficulties involved in effecting a military takeover, and instead relied upon trusted Welshmen to govern parts of the country in his name. Henry pulled the strings of these puppet princes, setting them up and plucking them down at will. Control of Deheubarth had passed into the hands of the princely house of Powys, while cautious Anglo-Norman advances were made on the fringes of native territory.

The great lordship of Pembroke was no longer held by the Montgomery family after Roger's son, Arnulf, became involved in a rebellion against the king, and it was divided up like an English shire controlled by lesser lords. An influx of Flemish settlers around c1108 further strengthened the Anglo-Norman grip on south Pembrokeshire. Their leaders included Wizo, Letard and Tancard, who established bases at Wiston, Letterston, and Haverfordwest. The northern boundary of this 'Little England beyond Wales' was defended by a string of castles from Roch in the west to Narberth in the east, and formed a buffer zone latterly known as The Landsker. From the West Country Robert fitz Martin came and established the lordship of Cemais centred on a new castle at Nevern, and Gerald de Windsor (constable of Pembroke after Arnulf's fall) built outposts at Carew and further afield at Cenarth Bychan in the Teifi valley. Further east, Norman bases were established at Kidwelly (1106) and Llandovery (by 1116), and the old fort at Rhydygors was either rebuilt or, more likely, replaced by a nearby site under royal control at Carmarthen.

Gerald's stronghold at Cenarth Bychan has never been located (though the most likely candidate is Cilgerran), and it was here

that he kept his family and valued possessions for safekeeping. However, he did not count on the lustful intrepidity of Owain ap Cadwgan (d.1116), son of the prince of Powys, who broke into the castle in 1109 and kidnapped Gerald's wife.

This bit of rape and pillage did not go down well with King Henry, who used the event as an excuse to punish Owain's father by dispossessing him of Ceredigion. Henry granted the land to Gilbert fitz Richard (d.c1115) of the powerful Suffolk house of Clare, and Earl Gilbert straightaway built castles at Aberystwyth and Cardigan. Although the Chronicles mention only these two sites at first, it is clear from later entries that Gilbert and his subordinates built castles in all but one of the ten *commotes* in Ceredigion; some of the names of these followers are commemorated by the castles they built – Walter's Castle (Castell Gwallter) Humfrey's Castle, and Stephen's Castle (Llanbedr Pont Steffan).

During these years the dispossessed heir of Rhys ap Tewdwr, Gruffudd ap Rhys (d.1137) made periodic efforts to strike back

Family tree of the main members of the Royal House of Deheubarth.

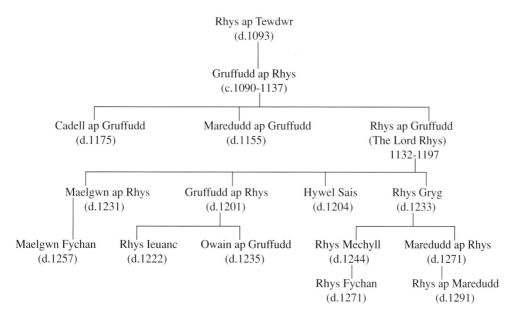

at the Norman and Welsh interlopers. In 1116 he attacked and burned Narberth, Llandovery and Swansea. King Henry responded by allowing trusted Welshmen to defend his castles. After failing to take Carmarthen, Gruffudd attacked Blaenporth and Ystrad Peithyll, but the subsequent raid on Aberystwyth went disastrously wrong when the garrison secretly received reinforcements. Tragedy struck again when Gruffudd's wife Gwenllian was killed in battle near Kidwelly in 1136.

When Gruffudd died, Ceredigion was already under threat from another invader – the house of Gwynedd, under the energetic leadership of the brothers Cadwaladr (d.1172) and Owain Gwynedd (d.1170). Cadwaladr had the heir to Deheubarth, Anarawd, murdered in 1143, and it was not until 1146 that the tide began to turn. Cadell ap Gruffudd (d.1175) and his younger brothers, Maredudd (d.1155) and Rhys (d.1197), began to strike out and reclaim the family lands lost to the Normans and Welsh alike. Cadell seized the de Clare castle of Dinweiler, Llansteffan, and (the most tempting target of all) the royal fortress of Carmarthen. The Welsh army moved on to the Landsker and captured Wiston, and within four years the triumvirate had won back Ceredigion from the princes of Gwynedd with the exception of the lone northern outpost of Castell Gwallter. But their triumph was short-lived; in the same year (1151) Cadell was assaulted and crippled by a gang of soldiers from Tenby. The mantle of leadership passed to Maredudd, and when he died just four years later, the hopes of Deheubarth rested with Rhys ap Gruffudd.

DEHEUBARTH UNDER THE LORD RHYS.

The house of Deheubarth reached its apogee under the firm and largely effective rule of Rhys ap Gruffudd (c1132-1197), known to his contemporaries as Lord ('Arglwydd') Rhys. By the last quarter of the twelfth century he was the most outstanding prince of native Wales and his vigorous defence of Welsh lands and culture against the seemingly unstoppable Anglo-Norman incursions has prompted some modern historians to claim that, without his efforts, west Wales would not be a Welsh-speaking area today.

Rhys's reign began auspiciously enough, by defeating an attempt by Owain Gwynedd to regain Ceredigion. His stand-off against King Henry II (1154-89) was less successful, and the appearance of a large army in 1158 forced Rhys into submission. Roger de Clare (d.1173) thought the time was ripe to press his claim on Ceredigion, and he took over the major castles there then under Welsh control. Rhys's patience snapped when another Norman lord began encroaching on his eastern frontier, and he retaliated by capturing Llandovery and all the castles in Ceredigion. It took the arrival of another big army to bring Rhys to heel, but the lesson was obviously not learnt and the following year (1159) more castles were burnt, and yet another royal army prompted a truce. In 1164 Rhys embarked on a violent crusade against the Anglo-Norman settlers and destroyed the unlocated de Clare outposts of 'Aber-rheidol' and 'Mabwynion', and reclaimed Ceredigion by '*inflicting repeated slaughters and conflagration and despoilings upon the Flemings*'.

King Henry could not ignore this continual truce-breaking indefinitely, and the following year he assembled a vast army to '*annihilate all Welshmen*' as the Chronicles claim. In the event, Rhys joined forces with Owain Gwynedd and the lesser princes, and watched Henry's great venture fizzle out in the moors and bogs of the Berwyn mountains. The summer weather could be just as unpredictable in the twelfth century! On his way home Rhys stopped off at Cardigan and flattened the castle.

By this time Henry must have realised that Wales could only be overcome with vast amounts of money and manpower. The Anglo-Norman conquests in Ireland were draining resources and his complicity in the murder of Archbishop Becket brought the king's authority to a low ebb. To defuse the situation in west Wales Henry came to terms with Rhys, appointing him 'Justice of South Wales'; and for almost twenty years the truce worked, ushering in a relatively stable and peaceful period. Rhys rebuilt the shattered walls of Cardigan and held the first recorded *Eisteddfod* there in 1176. With the Normans off his back he could even indulge in a bit of land-grabbing himself, building Rhayader castle in 1177 to bring part of mid Wales under his sway. In 1188 Rhys played host to Archbishop Baldwin, who was travelling through the country recruiting volunteers for the Third Crusade. Among the party was a scribe of mixed Norman and Welsh parentage, one Gerald de Barri (c1146-1223), better known as Giraldus Cambrensis, 'Gerald of Wales'. Gerald's writings allow us a vivid glimpse into the life, society and landscape of twelfth century Wales and Ireland.

The cordial relationship between Lord Rhys and Henry II came to an abrupt end on the king's death in 1189. Snubbed by the royal officials of the absent Richard I, Rhys went on the warpath again, and over the next ten years the Chronicles record an impressive list of castles captured and destroyed by the Welsh. But behind this saga of altruistic struggles is a squalid tale of family feuds and sibling rivalries between Rhys's innumerable offspring. Under Welsh law all sons had the right to an equal share of an inheritance and, while this had less effect than it might appear (given the high mortality rate – natural or otherwise – among the ruling classes), in Rhys's case it proved disastrous. At one point he was even incarcerated in Nevern castle by a rebellious faction of his family.

In 1197 plague swept through the land and the most noble victim was the great Rhys himself. It is not inconceivable that he died of natural causes, for he was about sixty-five, a ripe old age by Medieval standards. The prince was laid to rest at St David's cathedral where a fine stone effigy (carved some two centuries later) can still be seen. Over the

Profile of a Prince? The reputed tomb effigy of The Lord Rhys at St David's Cathedral.

anachronistic suit of armour is a surcoat emblazoned with the lion rampart crest of Deheubarth.

GWYNEDD ASCENDANT.

With Rhys's death the power and prestige of Deheubarth waned for good. It became a 'kingdom of many memories' as the territory was split up and ruled by his numerous heirs, at odds with each other and changing loyalties for material advantage. Maelgwn ap Rhys (d.1231) even went so far as to sell Cardigan castle *'the lock and stay of all Wales'* to King John (1199-1216) for a paltry sum, rather than allow his hated brother Gruffudd (d.1201) to claim rightful possession. This period witnessed the greatest threat to native west Wales and it was only the king's political troubles, coupled with the emergence of a strong national leader, that prevented a complete English takeover. The balance of power now shifted to the north, as Llywelyn Fawr, 'The Great', (1173-1240) began to extend his powerbase from Gwynedd and bring the lesser Welsh lords under his control.

The quarrelsome offspring of the Lord Rhys posed few problems for the ambitious prince. Maelgwn vigorously resisted any outside interference and in 1208 opted for a scorched-earth policy, destroying his important Ceredigion castles to prevent Llywelyn occupying them. In spite of this, Llywelyn wrested control away from Maelgwn and granted the land to his more pliable nephews. Maelgwn attempted to regain Ceredigion with the help of an English army, but when King John decided to build a castle at Aberystwyth, the blatant encroachment of royal authority proved too much; Maelgwn changed allegiance, joined forces with Llywelyn, and destroyed the castle.

Llywelyn now took full advantage of the deteriorating relationship between John and the barons to reassert Welsh independence by fire and sword. The *Brut* records a major Welsh offensive in 1215 when the castles of Cardigan, Carmarthen, Cilgerran, Kidwelly, Laugharne, Llansteffan, Narberth, Newport, Maenclochog and St Clears were taken and destroyed. The following year Llywelyn further demonstrated his authority over the Welsh princelings by convening a meeting at Aberdyfi and dividing the contested territories of Deheubarth among the Lord Rhys's heirs. In 1216 another son of the Lord Rhys, Rhys Gryg (d.1233), briefly reintegrated Gower with Deheubarth and evicted all the English settlers from the peninsula.

Nevertheless, significant gains were made by the English during this turbulent period and in 1223 William Marshal II (d.1231) seized control of Cardigan, Carmarthen and Cilgerran, and at the latter site began a rebuilding programme that made even the chronicler of the *Brut* sit up and take notice. The loss of the main Welsh leaders was a further blow; Maelgwn died in 1231, Rhys

Gryg two years later, and then the great Llywelyn passed away in 1240.

King Henry III (1216-72) may well have believed that it was only a matter of time before royal authority extended throughout Wales, for Llywelyn's heir, Dafydd, died in 1246 and the extensive territories were split up among his heirs. However, the king could not have counted on the luck, foresight and ambitions of Dafydd's nephew, Llywelyn ap Gruffudd (d.1282) who, in a few short years, clawed back all the territories (and more) held by his famous grandfather. Like his namesake, Llywelyn exploited the king's troubles at home (the Barons' War) to encroach on more land and bring the lesser princes under his control. In 1257 he joined forces with Maredudd ap Rhys Gryg (d.1271) and led a devastating raid through Deheubarth, burning the castles and towns of Laugharne, Llansteffan, Narberth, Newport and Maenclochog. He brought war to the very gates of Haverfordwest and may even

A modern memorial marks the site where Llywelyn ap Gruffudd died.

14

have contemplated an invasion of the rich agricultural lands of Glamorgan.

Unfortunately Llywelyn was not as tactful (or ruthless) as his grandfather had been in dealing with his allies, and he created numerous enemies – even among his own family. Llywelyn's treatment of Maredudd, in particular, was to have serious repercussions for Welsh supremacy in west Wales. Having first supported the prince, Maredudd was rewarded with control of Dinefwr in place of Rhys Fychan (d.1271) who had sided with King Henry. However, when Rhys renewed his old loyalties, Llywelyn reinstated him in Dinefwr, leaving the ousted Maredudd simmering with resentment.

FALL AND RISE: LLYWELYN THE LAST AND OWAIN GLYNDŴR.

King Edward I (1272-1307) was a more calculating monarch than his father Henry III, and following his coronation he demanded the expected homage from his vassals. When Llywelyn demurred persistently, Edward led an army into Wales in 1276 to force his submission. Rhys Fychan, lord of Dinefwr, and Maredudd, lord of Dryslwyn, had died within weeks of each other, but the family feud passed to their respective heirs, Rhys Wyndod (d.1302) and Rhys ap Maredudd (d.1291). The latter had no strong patriotic feelings towards Llywelyn, and when the royal armies moved against the prince, Rhys submitted to the king and helped the English forces subdue the lesser Welsh rulers of Deheubarth. Rhys kept his father's castle at Dryslwyn, but his hopes of gaining Dinefwr were dashed when it was taken over by the king. In north Wales the Treaty of Aberconwy stripped Llywelyn of much of his territorial gains, though it still left him with the hollow title of 'Prince of Wales'. Within five years rebellion flared again, this time prompted by Llywelyn's over-ambitious brother Dafydd (d.1283). Edward swiftly retaliated and by the end of the year Llywelyn was dead and Welsh resistance all but finished.

In Deheubarth the king's loyal ally, Rhys ap Maredudd, still ruled in Dryslwyn, but after a few years of chaffing against the restrictive administration and interference of Crown officials, the discontented lord started an uprising in the autumn of 1287. Rhys attacked and seized the neighbouring strongholds of Llandovery, Dinefwr and Carreg Cennen; but against the organised might of King Edward's military machine the uprising was doomed to failure. After a three week siege Dryslwyn fell, and Rhys escaped to Newcastle Emlyn before that too, was retaken. The fugitive was finally hunted down by his own kinsmen in April 1292, condemned as a traitor, and brutally executed at York.

A more serious uprising in 1294 by Madog ap Llywelyn, a scion of the house of Gwynedd, severely tested Edward's iron grip on Wales, but it was ultimately just as fruitless as Rhys's rebellion and its effect was felt most in north Wales. English control was secure and unchallenged in the west. The remaining Welsh lands and castles were in royal hands and administered from shire bases at Cardigan and Carmarthen. Other territories were controlled by Marcher Lords who generally had large estates elsewhere in the country. In time the various lordships were ruled by absentee landlords who would lease out the land, or grant the castles as dowries, gifts, and rewards for loyal service.

During the fourteenth and fifteenth centuries many Welshmen chose to throw in their lot with the English and find work as administrators, soldiers, constables and sheriffs, and while this may have provoked resentment among their neighbours, at least there were benefits to be gained. Gruffudd ap Nicholas of Llandeilo was one such ambitious landowner who laid the foundations of his family's subsequent rise to fame and fortune.

The role of the castle had changed too, and the introduction of a decisive new military factor – artillery – was to have a profound effect on the future development of fortifications. Castles still functioned primarily as fortified residences, but there was a greater emphasis on national, rather than just individual, defence. During the Hundred Years' War with France, Edward III (1327-77) ordered many of the Welsh castles to be refortified in case of attack. The attack, when it did come, was from an unexpectedly closer source.

At the beginning of the fifteenth century a shattering event brought the great fortresses back into the limelight, and severely tested the seemingly implacable English hold on Wales. What began as a boundary dispute between two wealthy landowners in mid Wales swiftly escalated into a national uprising led by the charismatic Owain Glyndŵr (c1354-1416). By 1405 most of the country was under his control and, prompted by bards and cautious allies, Owain could dream of a tripartite division of Britain with himself ruling all Wales and the Marches.

Owain's army appeared unstoppable. Most of the main castles were captured, Welsh parliaments were held at Machynlleth and Harlech, and Glyndŵr claimed the justified title of Prince of Wales. He even formed an alliance with France and led a troop of mercenaries across country as far as Worcester in 1405. But gradually the successes turned to defeats, his allies faded away, and royal forces under Henry IV (1399-1413) gained ground. The revolt petered out within a few years and harsh restrictive laws against Welshmen came into force. Owain's death is shrouded in mystery but it is held that he spent his remaining days in his daughter's home in a quiet Herefordshire valley.

CIVIL WARS AND GUNPOWDER.

There is an apocryphal story that Owain Glyndŵr encountered the Abbot of Valle Crucis on an early morning walk. 'You are up betimes, Master Abbot' said Owain, 'Nay . . . it is you who have risen too early . . . by a hundred years'. The reference is to Henry Tudor (1485-1509), Earl of Richmond, a descendant of a Welsh family, who seized the Crown in 1485. King Henry's link to the royal line was fairly tenuous, but the Tudors

ruled England for the next 120 years, ruthlessly stamping out any rival claimants. Henry was born in 1457 in the great Lancastrian fortress of Pembroke, then held by his uncle Jasper Tudor. The civil wars 'of the Roses' that fragmented society in the mid-fifteenth century witnessed a major casualty among the castles of west Wales. Carreg Cennen was held by a Lancastrian force under Gruffudd ap Nicholas, but following the Yorkist victory at Mortimer's Cross, the castle was surrendered and demolished.

For many historians the accession of Henry VII marks a convenient, if unrealistic, cut-off point for the Middle Ages, and certainly by then the age of the great feudal fortresses was over. For more than four centuries they had played a vital role in supporting (or undermining) the ruling elite of the land, but castles were now just antiquated residences or decaying properties. Military architecture had dramatically changed to keep pace with the increased use of artillery, and the fortifications constructed from the sixteenth century onwards cannot be called castles, and are beyond the scope of this book.

But the old castles were suddenly and unexpectedly recalled to duty, as relations between Parliament and King Charles I (1625-49) deteriorated from bad to worse. With the outbreak of civil war in 1644 many old strongholds were reused in the struggle and though they were greatly outmoded by the standards of the day, they weathered the storm with a solidity that would have made their builders proud.

More castles and fortified houses were used in the west than in any other part of Wales during the conflict. Some were provided with additional earthwork defences for the benefit of guns and cannons, and these outworks can still be seen at Carew, Manorbier, and Newcastle Emlyn. However, the greatest damage to these venerable buildings was not caused by Roundhead or Cavalier bombardment during a siege, but by the deliberate 'slighting' or demolition, subsequently carried out by the victorious

Parliamentarians. This varied from knocking down a parapet or a bit of the gate, to wholesale destruction; anything in fact that would render the building incapable of being used against the State in future.

POET, PAINTER AND ANTIQUARIAN.

By the end of the seventeenth century interest in the architectural heritage of Britain was gathering pace, and the mouldering castle became one of the prime targets for the proliferating breed of antiquarian. There had of course been earlier devotees of Medieval architecture – Gerald of Wales was writing about castles when they were still a living part of the landscape. But the first antiquarian to devote some attention to the subject was John Leland (c1506-52), who tracked through the country in the late 1530s, jotting down notes on anything that took his historical fancy. The individual descriptions in his 'Itinerary' however, are written in archaic English and tend to be rather succinct; but at least the notes allow a glimpse of the condition of the castles at the time.

George Owen (c1552-1613) of Henllys published a valuable 'Description of Penbrookshire' in 1603 which contains a mine of information for modern historians, though there are unfortunately few detailed notes on the individual castles. Edward Llwyd (1660-1709) was perhaps the first serious antiquarian to have a more active interest in Welsh archaeology, and he sent out questionnaires to various correspondents requesting information on local sites. A generation or so later, and Samuel and Nathaniel Buck travelled across Britain collecting material for a series of finely detailed copper plate etchings of castles and abbeys. Their work is still used in books today, and serves not only to record the buildings as they stood in the mid-eighteenth century, but also indicates the degree of fairly meticulous recording that was not to reappear until more recent times.

By the early nineteenth century, travellers, artists and guidebook writers were tramping the Welsh countryside in increasing numbers in search of the 'Romantic' landscape to praise in verse and line. Aside from these tour guides, much useful information on castles can be gleaned from a number of county surveys, of which the most important are Samuel Meyrick's 'History and Antiquities of the County of Cardigan' (1809) and Richard Fenton's 'Historical Tour

One of the numerous etchings of antiquities produced by the Buck brothers in the 1740s.

through Pembrokeshire' (c1811). In the early part of this century the Royal Commission on Ancient and Historical Monuments (RCAHM) was formed to record the archaeological heritage of Wales, and the published Inventories of Carmarthen (1917) and Pembroke (1925) are still standard reference sources. Today, survey and recording work is still carried out by the RCAHM and also by the Dyfed Archaeological Trust, which was founded in 1974-6. New county histories of Cardiganshire and Pembrokeshire are currently being researched.

PRESERVING THE PAST FOR THE FUTURE.

Conserving the remains of a castle was never much of a concern to early tourists, and it was quite common for the crumbling ruin to be helped to crumble even faster by stone robbers. Definite steps to maintain the buildings only really took shape in the late nineteenth century, with the establishment of the Ancient Monuments Board in 1882. For much of the time it was up to the discretion of private landowners to carry out essential repairs whenever necessary. Lord Cawdor did so at Carreg Cennen and Kidwelly, and J.R. Cobb carried out extensive works at Pembroke and Manorbier in the 1880s.

The function of the Ancient Monuments Board was eventually taken over by CADW: Welsh Historic Monuments, and CADW not only continues to repair monuments already in State Guardianship, but also takes over the maintenance of sites in private ownership (such as the recently acquired Wiston and Carswell). Renovation work on a large castle can take many years to complete. Purists may object to the sterile end result – neatly mown lawns and stark re-pointed walls devoid of ivy – but at least the structure can be seen and analysed. Excavations have been vital in recovering the plans of Aberystwyth and Dryslwyn, and would also be necessary at some future date to assist in the interpretation of Cardigan, Narberth and Newcastle Emlyn.

In west Wales today about seventeen castles are in State Guardianship and in Local Authority control, with a handful maintained by private owners. Many more crumble away uncared for, shrouded by weeds and bushes, in the corner of a field or a tangled forest.

Before and after: conservation work reveals the glory of Dinefwr Castle.

EARTH AND TIMBER CASTLES

A CONSERVATIVE estimate of the number of castles in west Wales (excluding lost or unlocated sites) indicates a total of about 153, and of this number 112 are earthwork fortifications with few, if any, signs of masonry defences. Stone was a time-consuming and costly material to use, and the majority of castles constructed between the end of the eleventh century, and the early years of the thirteenth century, relied on earthen defences supplemented with timber stockades and towers.

By today all the woodwork has decayed away, leaving only grassy mounds and banks to mark the site. To envisage the appearance of the vanished timber superstructure we must rely on rare contemporary documentation, the results of modern excavations, and a good deal of imagination. Unfortunately the evidence gleaned from archaeological work in this area is woefully inadequate, and therefore we must depend on the results gained from other sites in Wales and beyond, to build up our picture.

MOTTES

The Normans used two distinct types of castle in their campaigns, of which the most numerous and familiar is known as a **motte and bailey**. The motte is a conical mound of earth and rubble shaped like an overturned bowl, which was designed solely to support a wooden tower. The base of the mound was encircled by a deep ditch, and there was sometimes an additional outer defence work, called a **counterscarp** bank, around the rim of the ditch to increase the obstacles facing any attacker.

A motte may be a wholly man-made mound, but usually the builders relied upon shaping and scarping a natural hillock or ridge into the required shape. In west Wales

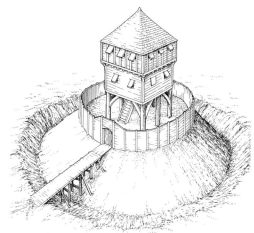

A reconstruction of a motte castle, showing one interpretation of the original appearance of a timber keep.

mottes vary in size from tiny tumps 1m high to substantial mounds over 12m in height. Additional buildings necessary for the running of a military station – including stores, stables, barracks, workshops – were housed in an adjoining fortified courtyard, the **bailey**. Many mottes do not have a bailey, and the accommodation provided by such sites must have been very limited indeed. In some cases the bailey earthworks have been ploughed away, undefended buildings nearby have left no trace above ground. Perhaps it is more likely that small solitary mounds were just short-lived outposts set up to enable an invading warlord to 'get his foot in the door'.

The famous Bayeux Tapestry illustrates a group of local labourers building the Conqueror's castle at Hastings in 1066, under the watchful gaze of a Norman overseer. The mound is depicted in coloured bands which might represent alternating layers of beaten earth, gravel, stones etc. to create a stable internal structure. Intriguingly, the tapestry shows a palisade already in place on the summit; this could simply be artistic convention, but evidence from excavations has revealed that sometimes earth was heaped around the base of a finished tower erected on natural ground level.

In all likelihood the wooden components of the tower were prefabricated at a carpenter's yard and brought to the site to be re-assembled – a process for building timber-framed structures that lasted into fairly recent times. The tower was called a **donjon** – though today it is referred to as a **keep** – and it was intended to be used as a strong point and last refuge of the garrison during an attack. The only access to the keep was along a bridge or ramp crossing the ditch, and there was probably some form of drawbridge or gate to hinder any unwelcome visitor.

The absence of surviving woodwork at early castle sites makes any reconstruction highly conjectural, and we must turn to the Bayeux Tapestry to gain some ideas. The section of the tapestry depicting Rennes (Brittany) shows a stylised, but still recognisable, motte castle comprising a modest tower of at least two storeys with a peaked roof, standing within a palisade on the mound top.

A larger and more elaborate structure is indicated on the motte at Bayeux. The access ramp leads up to a projecting gatehouse, and there appears to be an external fighting platform at roof level. All the buildings shown on the tapestry are highly decorative and may be imaginative, rather than literal, depictions of the structures built in the French and British countryside. It is not improbable that some of the more important castles had large, elaborate, keeps with painted and carved decorations, but the vast majority must have been very plain and austere.

Arrangements inside the keep were probably similar to existing houses, with a storeroom at ground level, a hall or living-room on the first floor, and perhaps private chambers on the topmost level. Many modern reconstructions show motte towers with flat battlements, but this is completely unfeasible in the British climate; all the exposed surfaces must have been roofed over to prevent the rain from seeping into the rooms and rotting the walls.

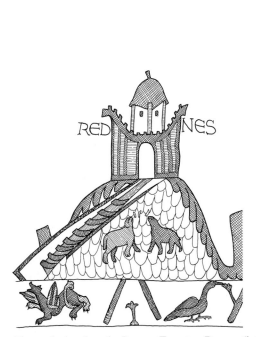 

Mottes depicted on the Bayeux Tapestry; Rennes (left) and Bayeux (right).

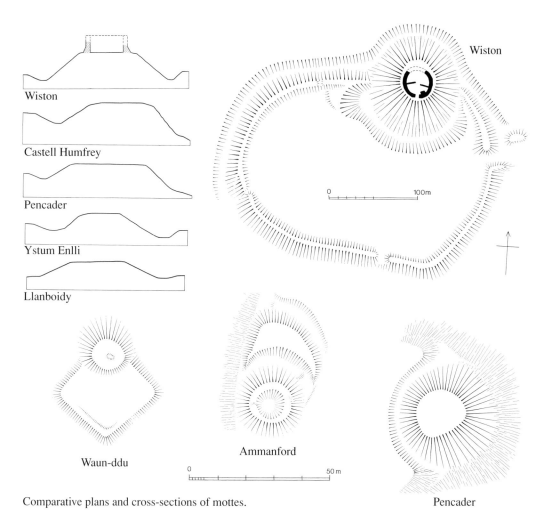

Comparative plans and cross-sections of mottes.

Dimensions of the towers would have varied with the size of the motte summit. At South Mimms (Hertfordshire) the timbers of a 10.7m square tower were found embedded in the motte, while a more modest mound at Abinger (Surrey) was crowned by a diminutive building 3m by 3.5m. The pattern of post holes revealed by excavation at Abinger indicated that the little tower was surrounded by a wooden palisade and wall-walk about 11m in diameter. The limited accommodation offered by Abinger is evidently at one end of the architectural scale, and the much larger summits of some castles – New Moat (19.6m) and Pencader (24.8m) for instance – hint at more ambitious buildings.

A contemporary account of a twelfth century motte in Flanders describes the tower containing a 'cellar' and granary on the ground floor, and a cluster of rooms on the upper floor, including a hall, larder and an 'inner room' warmed by a fire (presumably a brazier). On the topmost floor were 'garret rooms' and a chapel. This compact grouping of rooms is reflected in the discoveries made recently at Hen Domen near Montgomery. Only part of the bailey was excavated, but this was enough to reveal a dense concentration of timber buildings in a relatively small area, that had undergone extensive rebuilding and alteration between the eleventh and early thirteenth centuries.

RINGWORKS.

The other castle type built by the Normans is known as a **ringwork**, and consists of a circular courtyard enclosed with a strong bank and outer ditch. Where there was a suitable ridge or promontory site the builders needed only to dig the rampart on the most vulnerable level approach. Examples of such 'partial ringworks' can be seen at Parc-y-castell, Castell Gwynionydd, and Puncheston. There also exists another castle type usually termed a **ring-motte** which, as its name suggests, is a hybrid where the ringwork is raised above ground level so that it superficially resembles a motte. The mounds at Banc-y-bettws and Llanfyrnach may belong to this category.

Ringworks, like mottes, vary greatly in size and strength, from tiny enclosures such as Pengawsai (where the courtyard is no more than 8m by 10m), to the huge earthworks underlying the later stone castles at Kidwelly and Llawhaden. Ringworks began to be identified as a distinct type of Medieval fortification (rather than an exception) in the early part of this century. Previously they had been considered as Iron Age, Roman or Viking works. Even today, understandable confusion exists over their identification because of the similarity between genuine Medieval enclosures and small hillforts of Iron Age date. Some included here could in fact be Prehistoric

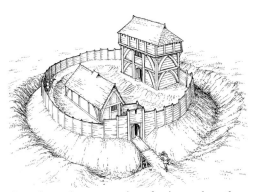

A conjectural reconstruction of a ringwork castle. This is based on Garn Fawr, where the flattening of the rampart on the uphill side suggests the former existence of a wooden tower (as shown).

earthworks. Nevertheless, the distinguishing factor is that Medieval sites tend to have fairly massive defences in relation to the small area enclosed.

Of the 112 earthwork castles in west Wales, about 39 can be classed as ringworks, and a further 12 can be detected under later stonework. It is interesting to note that many stone castles developed from this type rather than mottes. The archaeology of ringworks in Wales is better understood thanks to a number of important excavations carried out over the past hundred years. The earliest was in 1898 at Bishopston Old Castle (Gower), where traces of a timber palisade and walkway were found along the top of the rampart. In 1960 another Gower ringwork on Penmaen Burrows yielded evidence of a 6m square gatetower straddling an entrance gap in the bank. At some stage the tower was burnt down, and then the domestic accommodation was transferred to a simple drystone hall in the courtyard.

In the 1950s, excavations at Aberystwyth uncovered numerous post holes of vanished buildings within the ring, and the remains of a drystone entrance passage. Excavations at Sully (1963-69) and Rumney (1980-81) in Glamorgan, revealed the foundations of large wooden halls within the enclosures, and the ruins of later stone towers positioned close to the entrances. Even at some unexcavated sites it may be possible to detect the former presence of stone or timber towers by the thickening of the rampart, to form a building platform (as at Banc-y-bettws and Garn Fawr).

Whenever possible the builders of mottes and ringworks took advantage of pre-existing fortifications to bolster the defences. West Wales has a few examples of such 'hermit crab' castles, including Llansteffan and Rudbaxton Rath (both ringworks nestling inside Iron Age hillforts), and Waun-ddu (a motte on the corner of a Roman camp). Caer Penrhos ringwork lies within a hilltop enclosure which may well be a Prehistoric fort, though some experts think it is just an abnormally large bailey.

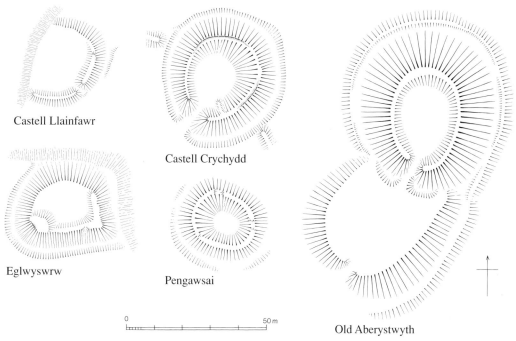

Castell Llainfawr

Castell Crychydd

Eglwyswrw

Pengawsai

Old Aberystwyth

0   50 m

Comparative plans of ringworks.

The huge twelfth century motte at Wiston supports a later shell-keep.

23

Most of these early castles left little trace on contemporary history and only in rare cases do we know who they were built by, or for how long they were occupied. The majority were built during the late eleventh to the early thirteenth centuries, and after 1200 new foundations were rare as stone fortifications became more widespread. However, this does not mean that the old castles were abandoned; many lingered on as temporarily occupied bases in times of unrest, or as semi-fortified manor houses. In 1225 Henry III ordered landowners in the Vale of Montgomery to *'have their mottes defended with good bretaches for their own safety and defence'*. A 'bretach' or brattice was a widely used term to describe some form of timber defence work such as a palisade or fighting gallery. The keep at Shrewsbury was still made of timber as late as 1270 when it collapsed in a storm, and the 'house' at Trefilan burnt in 1282 may have been the motte.

The most noteworthy example of the late use of mottes is Sycharth (Denbighshire), home of Owain Glyndŵr. Archaeologists have discovered the footings of two timber-framed buildings on the 25m top of the Norman motte, the largest measuring about 5.3m by 9.1m. Owain's home, praised by the court poet Iolo Goch as *'a fine wooden house on the top of a green hill'* was razed to the ground by Prince Henry in 1403.

GAZETTEER

The following gazetteer contains a list of the earth and timber castles in west Wales, along with brief information on some unlocated and rejected sites. Reference should also be made to Llandovery, Nevern and Wiston in the next section, which are predominately earthwork sites, but have sufficient visible stonework to warrant an entry there. In contrast, sites like Eglwyswrw and Ystradmeurig which have some vestiges of masonry, are best dealt with in this section.

The large number of entries has meant keeping the text to a minimum and avoiding detailed access arrangements. Most of these castles are on private land, but those marked with an asterisk can be seen from nearby roads and paths, or may be accessible to the public. Entries have been arranged in alphabetical order under the town or village, unless the name of the castle is in fairly common usage (for example, Cenarth, rather than *Parc-y-domen*). Where the site has an alternative name, this is given after the map reference. Placename spellings were obtained from current OS maps. Vertical heights were taken from the top of the mound/bank to the lowest ground surface or bottom of the ditch. Most of the sites were inspected for this book, but where I have had to rely on previously published sources, the measurements are shown in italics.

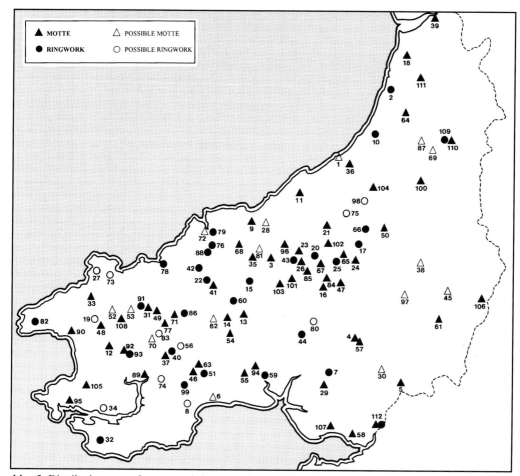

Map 2: Distribution map of mottes and ringworks in west Wales.

1 ABERAERON, Castell Cadwgan. Coastal erosion destroyed this site in the last century. Meyrick referred to it as a 'tumulus' (i.e. a motte), but a contemporary topographer, Samuel Lewis, described it as *'a small circular encampment'* which sounds more like a ringwork. The eponymous Cadwgan ruled Ceredigion from 1099 to 1110, and if any credence is attached to the placename, then this lost site could have been the first castle built by the Welsh.

2 ABERYSTWYTH (SN 585 790)*. Much of the early history of Aberystwyth is confused due to a change of placename, and the likelihood that more than two sites are involved. The first castle was built by Gilbert

fitz Richard in 1110 *'near the estuary of the river called Ystwyth'*, and a later entry in the *Brut* adds that it lay on top of a hill. There can be no doubt that this was the large ringwork and bailey at Rhydyfelin, about 3km south of the present town.

In 1116 Gruffudd ap Rhys attacked the castle, but his army was routed when a second Norman force led a surprise attack. Owain and Cadwaladr of Gwynedd burnt the fortress in 1136, but it must have been rebuilt by Cadwaladr because seven years later it was destroyed again in a family feud. Roger de Clare may have repaired it in 1158 (or else built a new castle), for in 1164 Lord Rhys destroyed an 'Aber Rheidol' castle. Llywelyn Fawr rebuilt Aberystwyth in 1208, and in

25

1211 King John started work on another castle which was destroyed by the Welsh within a few months.

A further reference to the castle in 1221 means that one of these sites had been rebuilt again. The next entry for Aberystwyth occurs in 1277, but this refers to the large stone castle beside the town, which will be dealt with in the next section.

From this confusing catalogue of destruction and rebuilding, all that can be safely claimed is that the castle of 1110-36 was the ringwork at Rhydyfelin. Here, on the brow of a steep hill overlooking the original estuary of the Ystwyth, a strong rampart *5m* high encloses an oval courtyard *20m* by *28m*, with a more weakly defended bailey on the south side. The ring is surrounded by a slight ditch and counterscarp bank, but the ditches have largely silted up. Excavations carried out in the 1950s revealed a scattering of post holes within the courtyard, and a stone-lined entrance passage. The later entries in the *Brut* could also refer to this site, or to lost castles in the adjacent Rheidol valley.

3 ADPAR (SN 309 409). This miserable specimen of a motte lies overgrown and hemmed in by buildings, on the opposite side of the river to Newcastle Emlyn. The damaged mound is between *3.6m* and *5.5m* high, and has no sign of a bailey. A small Welsh community here was developed as a borough by the Bishops of St David's.

4 ALLT-Y-FERIN (SN 522 233)*. Recent clearance of the undergrowth has enabled this impressive motte and bailey to be seen clearly for the first time in many years. It lies on a steep ridge above the Cothi river, and

Allt-y-ferin: an imaginary reconstruction of this Iron Age hillfort reused as a motte and bailey.

the defences consist of a strong bank, ditch and counterscarp bank crossing the neck of the promontory and isolating a triangular area of land. A large motte was formed by cutting a ditch through the rock and heaping the spoil over the end of the rampart.

The motte is between 4.9m and 7.6m high, with an 8m summit on which the brick foundations of a Victorian summer-house can be seen. The mound appears to be an addition to the rampart, and, in all likelihood, the builders made use of a pre-existing Iron Age hillfort. An inner ditch is probably Medieval, and was dug to prevent an enemy sneaking up from the more gentle slope at the tip of the ridge.

Allt-y-ferin has no recorded history, but it must have been built to control the surrounding commote of Gwidigada and (apart from the dubious site at Pantglas) is the only castle in this territory. It has also been identified as Dinweiler, an elusive site mentioned several times in the Chronicles, and which is thought to have lain in the adjacent commote of Mabudrud. Dinweiler was built by Gilbert de Clare in 1145-46, and the name of the nearby church of Llanfihangel *Llechweiler* strengthens the argument in favour of this site.

5 AMMANFORD (SN 624 125). A dense clump of rhododendrons hide the remains of this small motte and bailey. Natural slopes defend the west flank, and broad ditches formerly surrounded the other sides, but most have been filled in. The bailey is unusually small and narrow, and the stony motte is 5.5m high. The summit is 20m across and has a scooped out interior, so that the mound resembles a small ringwork superficially. The central crater is clearly a modern feature and may have been a fishpond or water tank.

6 AMROTH (SN 163 077). The present 'Amroth Castle' is a modern mansion on the coast, but antiquarian accounts refer to a possible motte on the hilltop south of the parish church. There are no obvious remains there now.

7 BANC-Y-BETTWS (SN 458 155)*. Close inspection reveals that this tree-covered mound is a ring-motte consisting of a mound 6.2m high and 17.5m across. The encircling rampart swells out on the southern edge as if to form the base for a wooden tower, but much of the eastern flank has been damaged by a modern quarry. A rock-cut ditch surrounds the site except on the north, where the farmer has filled it in.

8 BEGELLY (SN 117 072). An outlying stronghold of Manorbier lordship, the last remains of this castle were cleared away in 1955. According to the RCAHM it was a 'round camp' up to *2.4m* high and *50m* across, with a bailey on the north-west side. The dimensions suggest it was a ringwork rather than a motte.

9 BLAENPORTH (SN 266 488)*. This castle was built to control the commote of Iscoed by Gilbert fitz Richard in 1110, and was garrisoned by Flemish settlers from the surrounding countryside. In 1116 the Welsh army of Gruffudd ap Rhys rampaged through Ceredigion and burned the castle and adjoining town. One version of the *Brut* records how Gruffudd *'beseiged the tower throughout the day, and many from the tower were slain'*. Presumably the castle was rebuilt, but the chronicles make no further reference to Blaenporth.

Gilbert's castle is a large motte and bailey located on two promontories between stream valleys. The larger headland was utilised as a bailey of about two acres, defended by a rampart and ditch that has almost been ploughed out of existence. The smaller promontory was worked up into a steep motte 6.5m high, and is separated from the bailey by a deep natural gulley. On the summit is a curious egg-shaped earthwork 18m long by 12m wide, with a raised rim 2m thick. The sparse vegetation suggests the presence of buried stonework – but only excavation would confirm this.

10 CAER PENRHOS (SN 552 695)*. High on a windy hilltop above Llanrhystud lie the remains of this Welsh castle, built by Cadwaladr of Gwynedd in 1149. He passed control over to his son, Cadfan, but the following year a family feud broke out and his nephew, Hywel ap Owain, seized the castle. In 1151 Hywel was forced out by the Welsh princes of Deheubarth, but he returned with an army, slaughtered the garrison, and burnt the castle to the ground.

Llanrhystud is last mentioned in 1158 when it was captured and repaired by Roger de Clare; presumably it was among the unnamed castles destroyed by Lord Rhys later the same year. Cadwaladr's castle is a large ringwork of irregular shape, straddling the south-east side of a very large enclosure occupying the summit of the hill. This 'bailey' is almost certainly an Iron Age hillfort, and although it would have given additional protection to the ringwork, it is unlikely that a small Welsh garrison could have defended such a large area effectively.

The ringwork is surrounded by a strong rampart with an outer ditch on the west flank, and an entrance gap on the south leading across a rock-cut ditch into the 'bailey'. No trace of any buildings can be seen within the small courtyard, but the rampart in the north-east corner has been heightened and given a flat top, perhaps to support a small timber tower.

11 CAERWEDROS (SN 376 557)*. The Norman stronghold of Caerwedros was founded by Earl Gilbert in 1110 and destroyed by the princes of north Wales in 1136. Perhaps it was rebuilt, but there is no further documentation relating to its later history. Modern houses have encroached on the north side, but the motte itself is intact, and rises *3m* to a level summit *12m* across. The surviving stretch of ditch is encircled by a massive counterscarp bank, almost as high as the motte itself.

12 CAMROSE (SM 927 198)*. The tree-covered earthworks lie across the valley from the parish church, and a modern road separates the *4.8m* high motte from a small bailey. The Pembrokeshire historian, Richard Fenton, noted that the mound had been 'converted into a shrubbery with spiral walks around it' (c1811).

13 CASTELL BACH (SN 247 275). Dense undergrowth makes an interpretation of this site difficult at present, but it appears to be a motte built up over the end of a ridge, about 5m high, with a flat summit 13m across. Traces of a low rampart around the top suggest that it might be a worn down ring-motte.

14 CASTELL COSSAN (SN 202 268)*. Only an eroded fragment of a motte 3m high remains today, but traces of a wide, silted ditch indicate that it was once much larger. The little heap of layered rubble is just the stony core of the mound.

15 CASTELL CRYCHYDD (SN 261 348)*. Richard Fenton described this site as *'an encampment of oblong form with rounded angles, and a circular deep earthwork adjoining it at the east end'*. Turnip diggers had found bits of 'Roman' pottery in the adjacent fields, hinting that there was a Celtic settlement nearby (or more likely, the pottery was misattributed Medieval ware).

Castell Crychydd is a large and strong ringwork and bailey situated at the southern edge of the commote of Emlyn is Cych. In the twelfth century this became the lordship of Cilgerran. Probably the castle was built by the Normans to secure this part of the lordship, but during the reign of the Lord Rhys, Cilgerran was in Welsh hands and was only recovered by the Marshals in 1204-15 and 1223.

The defences consist of a very strong bank up to 5.4m high, enclosing a small oval courtyard 15m by 20m, with an entrance gap leading to the larger bailey. There are surface indications of a building, perhaps a tower, beside the entrance, and around the summit of the bank is a ruined stone wall. The bailey occupies a wide strip of sloping ground between the ringwork and a stream valley, with banks and ditches defending the vulnerable flanks. The open side above the valley has been damaged by quarrying, but there are signs that the bailey was enclosed by stone walls (unless the visible stonework is modern).

Without excavation it is impossible to date the masonry defences. It is probably secondary work, and may have been built by the Welsh in the late twelfth century or, more likely, by the English in the early thirteenth century.

16 CASTELL DU (SN 437 341). A small and well preserved motte on sloping ground near Pencader. The flat topped mound is *4.5m* high and *7.6m* across, with vestiges of a silted ditch on the uphill side.

17 CASTELL DOL-WLFF (SN 520 445), Castell Sant Esen. Mostly destroyed in 1968. This ringwork consisted of an oval enclosure with a *2m* high rampart and ditch on the north flank.

18 CASTELL GWALLTER (SN 622 868)*. High on a hill above the Lleri valley lie the remains of a large motte and bailey built by Walter de Bec around 1110. The castle was destroyed by Cadwaladr and Owain Gwynedd in 1136, but they rebuilt it and held it against the rightful rulers of Deheubarth until 1153. With its capture, the northern princes were expelled from Ceredigion, and the castle is mentioned no more in the Chronicles. Was it one of the anonymous sites refortified by Earl Roger de Clare in 1153? If so then it would have been destroyed by Lord Rhys in the same year.

The earthworks comprise a *4.5m* high motte surrounded by a ditch and counterscarp bank. This stands at one side of a large bailey about *150m* square, which has been subdivided by worn-down banks into smaller enclosures on either side of the mound. The complex nature of the earthworks might be explained as a Norman re-use of an Iron Age

site, but only excavation will provide an answer.

19 CASTELL GWILYM (SM 882 277)*, Castle Villa. On the edge of an escarpment is an oval enclosure up to *46m* across, and surrounded by a bank, ditch and counter-scarp. Earlier accounts mention an additional outer rampart. The site has been identified as a possible ringwork, but its size and multiple defences are more typical of an Iron Age fort.

20 CASTELL GWYNIONYDD (SN 424 420). This large partial ringwork lies on a steep slope above the Teifi valley and was probably the administrative centre of the commote of Gwynionydd. A broad ditch and strong rampart up to 3m high defends the only flank vulnerable to attack, and a slight gap in the bank marks the site of an entrance.

The nineteenth century historian, Samuel Meyrick, mentioned the *'ruins of the foundations of the keep'* which implies that some masonry remains were then visible. Nothing survives above ground today.

21 CASTELL HUMFREY (SN 441 476)*, Castell Hywel. Following Earl Gilbert's invasion of Ceredigion in 1110, the eponymous Humfrey seized the commote of Gwynionydd and built this strong castle on a ridge above the Clettwr valley. The end of the ridge was cut off by a deep ditch, and built up into a motte 6m high and 17m across, which

Castell Humfrey. Slight earthworks in front of the large motte suggest there was a bailey here, as shown in the reconstruction drawing.

has been dug into by treasure hunters. A low earthwork in the adjoining field could be an additional defensive bank, or the remains of a small bailey.

Humfrey's castle was burnt by Cadwaladr and Owain Gwynedd in 1137, and may have been left derelict until Owain's son, Hywel, rebuilt it in 1151. Seven years later Roger de Clare captured a number of strongholds, including Castell Humfrey, but within the same year the Welsh counter-attacked. A war band led by the Lord Rhys's nephew, *'made for Humfrey's castle, and slew the knights and other keepers who were there, and won huge spoils and steeds and armour'*. The unknown chronicler was perhaps exaggerating the outcome of the raid, or else the 'huge spoils' reflect Earl Roger's investment in his military venture.

22 CASTELL LLAINFAWR (SN 151 374)*. A weakly defended ringwork on marshy ground near Eglwyswrw. The enclosure is defended by a 2.8m high rampart curving around three sides. The outer ditch has silted up, and the remaining flank has only a boggy stream for protection. A gap in the middle of the bank could be an entrance, but looks more like a modern break.

23 CASTELL NANT-Y-GARAU (SN 369 421)*. This well-preserved motte lies in a field behind Penrhiw-llan village, and can be seen from a waymarked footpath. The mound rises to a maximum height of *4.2m* above a boggy ditch, and has a flat tree-covered summit *19.8m* across.

24 CASTELL NONNI (SN 495 399). A small, but well-preserved motte lying in a grove of trees beside a boggy stream. The mound rises *5m* above a silted ditch, with a flat summit *15m* across.

25 CASTELL PANT-Y-FEN (SN 462 401). An Iron Age hillfort or a Medieval ringwork? The clues are slight, but the small size and absence of any defences on the naturally strong side favour a Medieval date. A bank

and ditch 3.5m high encloses a circular area, 24m across, on a bluff above the Teifi. Part of the rampart (including the entrance) has been removed and the ditch filled in.

26 CASTELL PISTOG (SN 382 403)*. An overgrown motte on farmland overlooking the Teifi valley. The mound rises *6m* above an encircling ditch to a disturbed summit *16m* across. Recent examination of old aerial photographs has indicated the earthworks of a ploughed-out bailey on the east side.

27 CASTELL POETH (SM 897 377)*. In a field beside the Pwllderi road is a circular earthwork about 30m across, with an outer ditch. Richard Fenton thought this was a burial mound and saw 'fragments of urns', but the OS map marks it as an enclosure with an outer rampart (of a bailey?) on the east side. This could be an Iron Age fort or a Medieval ringwork, but the site is now so overgrown that little can be seen.

28 CASTELL PRIDD (SN 295 496). The last vestiges of this mound were removed in the 1930s. Samuel Meyrick referred to it as a 'tumulus' (i.e. a burial mound), and so it was probably a small motte.

29 CASTELL-Y-DOMEN (SN 436 126). A largely natural mound *9m* high, located in woodland on the edge of a steep drop to the Gwendraeth river. The motte is protected by a rock-cut ditch on the landward side.

30 CASTELL-Y-RHINGYLL (SN 578 148). There are antiquarian references to a possible mound at Castell-y-rhingyll, and another at nearby Castell-y-garreg – though only the placenames provide the most convincing evidence now. One of the presumed sites may have been the unlocated 'Luchewein' mentioned in 1206 and 1209.

31 CASTLEBYTHE (SN 021 290)*. One of a string of minor castles built to defend the foothills of the Preseli Mountains. This rather shapeless, tree-covered mound stands *3-6m* high, with an uneven summit *12m* across.

The ditch has been filled in, and there is no sign of a bailey (although the RCAHM report of 1925 mentions one).

32 CASTLEMARTIN (SR 915 984)*. Behind the little village is a circular earthwork *76m* across, enclosed by a weak rampart and a broad outer ditch. The site is poorly preserved and disturbed by later field boundaries, and looks more like an Iron Age site than a Medieval ringwork. The place is listed in a document of c1245, and John Leland mentioned *'vestiges of Martin Castle'*.

33 CASTLEMORRIS (SM 903 316). The remains of this motte were destroyed in the last century, and the skeleton of a man was found underneath it, raising the possibility that it was a re-used burial mound. Little is known of its history, but a reference in the Black Book of St Davids (1326) to the place being a seat of justice with a constable, might imply that the castle was still in use then.

34 CASTLE PILL (SM 918 064)*. On a rocky ridge high above Castle Pill inlet near Milford Haven lie the remains of an artillery fort built in 1643 during the Civil War. Such a fortification is outside the scope of this book, but the Elizabethan historian George Owen listed it as a castle some forty years before the outbreak of war. Richard Fenton described it as '*a mixture of ancient earthworks improved by more modern masonry*', but since his time the site has become very overgrown and damaged by agricultural activities.

Despite the undergrowth, it is still possible to make out a rounded enclosure defended on the weaker north and west sides by a 3m high rampart and outer ditch. The bank is faced with stonework in places, and at the eastern end, overlooking the valley, is a masonry tower or bastion of D-shape plan.

Presumably the masonry remains belong to the seventeenth century, but the rounded form of the enclosure is untypical of the defensive trends of the time, and could be an earlier ringwork. Royalist troops built the fort to break the Parliamentarian hold on Pembroke and the Haven. The incomplete fort was beseiged by land and sea in February 1644, and news of its capture prompted the disheartened Royalist garrison in Haverfordwest to desert.

35 CENARTH (SN 269 414)*, Parc-y-domen, Domen Fawr. A well-preserved motte now covered in trees, lying opposite the parish church. The flat topped mound is about *6m* high, but the surrounding ditch has silted up.

36 DINERTH (SN 495 624). Built by Gilbert fitz Richard in 1110 to control the commote of Anhuniog. It was burnt by the Welsh in 1136, and rebuilt by Roger de Clare in 1158. The castle may have been destroyed in the general campaign waged by the Lord Rhys the same year. It was back in Welsh hands by the close of the twelfth century, when Maelgwn seized Dinerth from his brother Gruffudd in 1199. Maelgwn finished building the defences four years later, but in 1208 he was forced to demolish the castle to prevent his enemy Llywelyn Fawr from occupying it. Dinerth makes no further appearance in the Chronicles, and it may be assumed that this demolition ended the effective life of the castle.

The site is now very overgrown, and lies on a rocky ridge between two deep valleys. The builders evidently carved up a natural outcrop to form the castle, and this explains the great size and irregularity of the earthworks. On the level eastern approach there is an outer bank and ditch, then an inner ditch fronting a huge mound over 8m high that looks like a motte, but is probably an unfinished rampart.

The summit of the ridge has been cut in two by a ditch, and the eastern half raised to form a motte 8m high, with a narrow top 5m by 9.8m. Judging from the surface indications there may have been a square stone tower here, one side having fallen into the stream below. The remainder of the ridge

Dinerth: A complex and unusual castle built on a rocky ridge in 1110.

slopes down to the stream, where several terraces may have accommodated residential buildings.

37 DINGSTOPPLE (SN 061 186). One of the smallest mottes in Wales, rising just 1.6m above an ill-defined, boggy ditch, to a summit barely 9m across. This unspectacular mound lies in a hollow on sloping ground, and could hardly have had much strategic value. This prompts the suspicion that it is not a motte castle in the usual sense, and might even have been a Prehistoric burial mound.

38 DOLAUCOTHI (SN 662 401)*. Beside Carreg Pumpsaint at the entrance to the Roman gold mines is a conical heap of rubble which looks very much like a motte. This may be taken as evidence that the Normans (or Welsh?) were reworking the mines, but the mound could be just an old spoil heap. Ongoing excavations may solve the riddle.

39 DOMEN LAS (SN 686 969)*. A few years after being expelled from Ceredigion, Owain Gwynedd attempted to reclaim the territory and met with Lord Rhys's army at Aberdyfi in 1156. Rhys *'raised a ditch to give battle'*, but the event did not develop beyond a show of strength. Owain retired, and Rhys replaced his temporary fortification with a castle, probably the motte now known as Domen Las. This was the *'castle of the Dyfi'* captured by Roger de Clare in 1158, and presumably destroyed by Rhys a few months later.

It is possible that 'Abereinion' castle mentioned in 1169 and 1206 may be Domen Las, since the river Einion joins the Dyfi nearby. The *4.2m* high motte has a summit *18.2m* across, and lies at the tip of a low ridge beside the estuary. The landward approach is guarded by a rock-cut ditch.

40 DRIM CASTLE (SN 064 196). On the edge of an escarpment above the Syfynwy valley is a small ringwork surrounded by a damaged rampart and outer ditch. This is probably a Medieval site, though there are several small Iron Age forts in the vicinity.

41 DYFFRYN-MAWR (SN 175 351). Lying on a headland between two streams, this odd earthwork is usually classed as a ringwork, but looks more like a mutilated motte. The tree covered mound rises 6.8m above a well-preserved ditch and counterscarp, and the foundations of a stone wall can be seen around the summit.

The interior is deeply cratered with an impossibly small habitation area – clearly there were no buildings here. The pit could be the work of modern 'treasure' hunters. An unofficial dig in 1920 revealed two post holes 0.3m square outside the wall, presumably either part of the pre-masonry defences, or the supports for an access ramp.

42 EGLWYSWRW (SN 139 383).

Although marked on OS maps as a 'motte and bailey', this is actually a small ringwork, with an internal area of about 20m by 26m, situated just west of the village. The weaker south and west sides are protected by a bank and ditch, with steep natural slopes on the north. The supposed motte is a stony mound that marks the remains of a tower not more than 7m square. Erosion has revealed one of the wall faces. This must have been the original seat of the manor of Eglwyswrw, held by the Cantington family, before it was moved 1km away to Court Farm, where traces of a later moat survive.

43 FELINCWRWS (SN 351 411).

A small, but strong partial ringwork on an overgrown headland above a tributary valley of the Teifi.

44 GARN FAWR (SN 398 238).

This large and well preserved ringwork lies on the edge of a steep valley north of Carmarthen. The ring bank is particularly strong on the uphill side, with a pronounced thickening that may have supported a wooden tower. The bank is 4m high and encloses a sloping courtyard 12m across with an entrance gap on the north-east side. The landowner has recently filled in part of the ditch.

The castle has no recorded history, but it must have been built to control the hill-country north of Carmarthen, and is only one of two sites in the large commote of Elfed. Until the last century the ruins of Llanfihangel Croesfeini church could be seen nearby, and some vague earthworks in an adjoining field (now much ploughed down) could be relics of an abortive Norman settlement. There was certainly a Christian centre here in the Dark Ages, and the 'croesfeini' or cross stones, were removed from here to Carmarthen museum some years ago.

Eglwyswrw: This conjectural reconstruction of the ringwork castle shows the little stone keep overlooking the presumed site of the entrance.

45 GLAN MYNYS (SN 731 326)*. From a distance this tree-covered mound looks like a perfect motte, but closer inspection reveals it to be a shapeless tump with no sign of any ditches. It could well be a natural feature.

46 GLYNPATEL (SN 128 142)*, Green Castle. Poorly located in a marshy valley below Crinow hamlet is a small motte, *4.5m* high and *9m* across. The mound is free from undergrowth, but rather worn down, and a slight ridge on the south side could be all that remains of a bailey.

47 GWYDDGRUG (SN 477 356). This has previously been classed as a motte and bailey, but the vague, mutilated remains now bear little resemblance to a Medieval site at all. On the edge of a steep slope is a shallow, rounded depression, perhaps the remains of a bailey bank or the edge of a ditch. Within this, and incorporated into a hedge, is a low heap of earth and pebbles that might be the last vestiges of a small motte. This site has been tentatively identified as the 'Gwyddgrug' destroyed by the Welsh in 1146, rather than the better-known Wyddgrug (Mold) in north Wales.

48 HAYSCASTLE (SM 895 256)*. Surviving vestiges suggest this was a large motte, at least 17m across; but half the tree-covered mound has been dug away in recent times. The north flank facing the road is virtually intact, and rises 4.6m above a boggy ditch. The place-name appears in the Black Book of St Davids (1326), though it is unsafe to infer that the castle was still in use then.

49 HENRY'S MOAT (SN 044 275)*. Fenton referred to this small motte as *'Castell Hendrev . . . a flat headed tumulus with a ditch around it'*, but the ditch has since been filled in, and one side of the mound has been damaged by a track. The name translates literally as 'old dwelling' (hen dre[f]), giving rise to the belief that it was the forerunner of New Moat. The motte can be seen from the churchyard, and where best preserved, stands 4.4m high with an uneven summit 10.7m across.

50 LAMPETER (SN 579 482)*, Stephen's Castle. Beside the college buildings is a tall, mutilated fragment of a motte almost *8m* high, but with no trace of a ditch or bailey. This is the 'Llansteffan' mentioned in 1137, an error for Castell Steffan, a name which commemorates its Norman builder. The castle of Mabwynion captured by the Welsh in 1164 may be another reference to this site.

51 LAMPETER VELFREY (SN 155 146)*, Castell Cynon. The end of a ridge north of the village has been scarped to form a large oval ringwork, with a *3.6m* high rampart and ditch on the west flank. The site is now covered with trees but can be seen from the road.

Along with the motte at nearby Glynpatel, this castle guarded the commote of Efelffre, which was eventually incorporated into the lordship of Narberth. In the late twelfth century Efelffre and neighbouring Ystlwyf were granted to Lord Rhys, and Castell Cynon would certainly have been manned (if not actually built) by the Welsh during their short-lived tenure.

52 LETTERSTON (SM 938 295), Parc Moat. According to the RCAHM (1925) this site was an eroded mound *91m* across, but in the 1960s it was said to be only *18m* across, and *1.8m* high, with slight traces of a ditch. Various accounts describe it as a burial mound, motte or ringwork, but I could not locate the site in 1997. The placename derives from a Flemish settler named Lettard (d.1137).

53 LITTLE NEWCASTLE (SM 980 289). The last remains of this castle were swept away in 1965, and Fenton described it as a *'large mount or tomen'*, which indicates it was a motte. However, the dimensions given by the RCAHM (*3m* high and *45m* across) rather suggest a ringwork – or else a severally flattened motte! It had a bailey on the west side and possibly some stone buildings, since the outlines of buried foundations were seen in 1914. The castle was in existence by c1200, when it was mentioned in the foundation charter of Pill priory.

54 LLANBOIDY (SN 219 231)*, Castell Mawr. This castle can be reached by a public footpath from the village green, and lies on a low ridge between two streams. The motte is 4.3m high with a summit diameter of 16m, and ploughing has reduced the encircling ditch to a shallow depression. More worrying is the continuing damage to the bailey, which now survives only as a vague rectangular platform.

55 LLANDDOWROR (SN 253 147)*. A natural hillock at the foot of sloping ground has been worked up into a feeble and ill-defined mound about *2m* high. The RCAHM report of 1914 suggests there was a bailey on the west side, but the surface indications are now too vague to be sure.

56 LLANDRE EGREMONT (SN 094 203)*. Built on the edge of a steep slope, this enclosure has every appearance of being a ringwork, except that the bank and ditch (now much ploughed down) enclose an almost square area, more reminiscent of a moated manor. It has been classed as such, but there are no water-filled ditches here. Perhaps Llandre was an unusual type of ringwork, like the one at Ystum Enlli.

57 LLANEGWAD (SN 517 214)*, Pen-y-cnap. This eroded and tree-covered motte was the 'castle of Llanegwad' captured by Rhys Ieuanc in 1203. No other documents mention the site, and it is not clear if this was an earlier outpost of English power in the Tywi valley, or a Welsh castle built during the family feuds after Lord Rhys's death. The mound is 6m high with an irregular summit 12m across. There are traces of drystone walls on the slopes, and the broad encircling ditch now only remains on the uphill side. This flank was further protected by a large triangular bailey noted by the RCAHM in 1917, but which no longer survives.

58 LLANELLI (SN 501 004)*. The strong-hold of the commote of Carnwyllion was a motte and bailey situated within an S-bend of the river Lliedi, but due to industrial growth in the nineteenth century, the river was diverted and the mound virtually submerged beneath the tinplate works reservoir. All that can be seen now is the bush-covered tip of the motte, garrisoned by ducks. Antiquarian records also mention a rectangular earthwork in the vicinity of John St. but whether this was a castle, moated manor, or even an earlier Roman fort, is now impossible to determine.

59 LLANFIHANGEL ABERCYWYN (SN 297 136)*, Castell Aber Taf. Along with Laugharne, this ringwork and bailey is a likely candidate for the unlocated 'Aber Cofwy' mention in 1116. It was owned by Robert Courtemain, but Henry I allowed a trusted Welshman, Bleddyn ap Cedifor, to hold it against the army of Gruffudd ap Rhys. The placename may derive from the estuaries of the Corran, Taf or Cywyn, which flow into Carmarthen Bay, but a direct identification is difficult. By 1171 the surrounding commote of Ystlwyf had been granted by Henry II to Lord Rhys, who in turn passed control over to his son, Hywel. The castle would surely have been used by the Welsh to control this outlying territory.

The castle makes no further appearance in recorded history, but the proximity of the ruined church of St Michael with its remarkable 'pilgrims' graves' suggests there was an attempt to found a settlement here.

When the RCAHM photographed the site earlier this century the earthworks were clearly visible, but now they are densely overgrown and practically inaccessible. The ringwork is about 4m high with a courtyard *22m* across. A ditch separates the oval bailey *27m* by *46m* on the east side. There is much stone rubble in the ringwork bank suggesting the former existence of masonry defences, but only clearance and detailed survey work would confirm this.

The castle lies on private land behind Trefenty Farm off the A40, but there is a public footpath to the ruined church.

60 LLANFYRNACH (SN 219 312)*. Dense undergrowth covers the remains of a possible ring-motte beside the church. The mound is about *6m* high and *18m* across, with a depressed summit. Where the vegetation allows, some tumbled stonework can be seen in the encircling bank.

61 LLANGADOG (SN 709 276)*, Castell Meurig. A textbook example of a motte and bailey, lying close to the A4069 south of the village. The mound was shaped from a natural rocky hillock and rises *9m* above a deep ditch that separates it from a large, oval bailey. Although the motte is covered with trees and a house sits in the bailey, the earthworks are otherwise very well preserved.

The castle is only mentioned as late as 1203 when it changed hands in the Welsh feuds that signified the collapse of Deheubarth. It was captured again in 1208 and burnt in 1209. Since it lay deep within contested Welsh territory, it may have been a native stronghold, or else an early Norman outpost re-used in the struggles.

62 LLANGLYDWEN (SN 177 268). Site of a vanished castle on a hill above the village. It is thought to have been a motte and bailey.

63 LLANGWATHEN (SN 134 153). This solitary motte was discovered in the early 1980s during the construction of a gas pipeline, and lies in a marshy valley near Narberth. The disturbed mound is *3m* high and *20m* across, and may be all that remains of a settlement mentioned in Medieval documents.

64 LLANILAR (SN 630 746)*, Pen-y-castell. In 1242, Maelgwn Fychan 'fortified' the castle of Garth Grugyn, an unlocated site which, presumably, lay near Crugyn township in the upper Ystwyth valley. A likely candidate for the site is Pen-y-castell, an unusual earthwork on a lofty hill above Llanilar. The summit has been shaped into an oval bailey with a massive rampart and counterscarp bank. This is separated from a motte by a deep rock-cut ditch (enlarged by modern quarrying). The motte lies at the most secure part of the site, but at a lower level; the summit is very uneven which suggests that the castle was never completed.

65 LLANLLWNI (SN 474 413)*. Church and castle occupy the summit of an isolated hill above the river Teifi. The motte is very overgrown and the ditch has been filled in on the west side. On the east side the ditch and counterscarp are well marked, and the motte rises 5.6m to a level summit 15m across. Beyond the ditch the ridge ends in a precipitous triangle of land that superficially resembles a bailey.

66 LLANWNEN (SN 533 472), Castell Du. A small ringwork located in woods on the banks of the river Grannell, just south of the village. The ditch has been largely filled in, but a *2m* high bank surrounds a small courtyard, defended on the east side by the natural slopes.

67 LLWYNBEDW (SN 432 397)*. A rather weak and shapeless motte 2.6m high, lying on enclosed, marshy ground below a farmyard. The mound is believed to have been lowered in height around 1880, and the surrounding ditch only survives on the west side.

68 LLWYNDYRIS (SN 237 433)*. A small motte hidden in bushes beside the A484 near Llechryd. The mound is built over a natural ridge beside the river Teifi, and has a summit *9m* across. On the landward side the mound is *4.5m* high, but the scarp is much higher towards the river.

69 LLWYN-GWYNAU (SN 669 635). On top of a hill beside Tregaron Bog, OS maps mark a 'motte', but all that now remains is a ploughed-down stony mound barely 1m high and 13m across. It could be the last vestige of a small motte or, more likely, a Prehistoric burial mound.

70 LLYS-Y-FRAN (SN 039242). A possible motte recorded by the RCAHM in 1925 no longer survives, and may have been destroyed with the construction of the adjacent reservoir.

71 MAENCLOCHOG (SN 083 272). All that remains of this important castle is the natural rock outcrop it stood upon. It was destroyed by Rhys Ieuanc in 1215, and again by Llywelyn in 1257, when the adjacent settlement was also razed. The castle, which had stone defences, according to tradition, was probably re-built and is mentioned in documents as late as 1376.

72 MANIAN-FAWR (SN 150 478)*. Marked on OS maps as a 'tumulus' or burial mound, this is perhaps a small motte, consisting of a natural outcrop *15m* by *30m*, defended by rock-cut scarps.

73 MANOROWEN (SM 942 367), Castle-martin. The end of a ridge overlooking Goodwick has been scarped into an oval platform *3m* high, but which is now overgrown and damaged. The defences on the landward side have been levelled. This could be a worn-down motte, though it has also been classed as a ringwork.

74 MINWEAR (SN 063 134). On the edge of a valley in Minwear woods is an oval enclosure 28m across, with a faint ditch on the west side. Where best preserved, the rampart is 1.8m high, but the whole site has been damaged by ploughing and is poorly preserved. Only excavation will confirm if this is a ringwork or an Iron Age fort.

75 MOYDDIN-FACH (SN 475 514). The end of a ridge above the Grannell stream has been shaped into a small enclosure defended by a weak bank and ditch. This might be an Iron Age site rather than a Medieval ringwork.

76 NANTPERCHELLAN (SN 172 434). The very overgrown tip of a ridge between two valleys is defended by a strong rampart about *2.4m* high, enclosing a courtyard about *48m* across. Again, this could be an Iron Age site.

77 NEW MOAT (SN 063 253)*. The little village of New Moat was once an important borough under the control of the Bishops of St Davids, and was probably founded some time in the late twelfth century. It was certainly here by c1200 when the placename (Nova Mota) is mentioned in the foundation charter of Pill priory, and some think it may have replaced an older centre at nearby Henry's Moat, or another castle by the church, where faint earthworks have been recorded.

The fledgling settlement was protected by a motte and bailey, and a reference in the charter to an 'east gate' might suggest there were some defences or, more likely, the town was initially accommodated within the large bailey. The outer earthworks of the bailey are now poorly preserved, but the line is marked by hedge banks along the roadside. On the opposite side a marshy stream gave some additional defence. The tree-covered motte is still very prominent, and rises 5.2m above a flooded ditch to a level summit 19.7m across. A stone roofing slate was found on the motte during survey work.

78 NEWPORT (SN 058 396)*. Below the town on the banks of the Nevern estuary are the remains of a partial ringwork, now very overgrown and damaged. The ditch is well marked, and where best preserved the rampart rises 3.5m to enclose a sloping courtyard with an open side facing the river. This is probably a Medieval rather than an Iron Age site, but its proximity to the later stone castle of Newport (which overlies a large ringwork), brings into question the origin of the town.

William fitz Martin abandoned Nevern sometime between 1191 and 1215 (when a castle at Newport is first mentioned). This site could have been William's first choice for a new settlement, giving rise to the Welsh placename Trefdraeth ('town on the sands'), before he relocated a little way inland. However, this small ringwork seems a poor substitute for the much larger stronghold at Nevern, and it might instead have been an earlier Norman base. Only future excavation might reveal the answer.

79 OLD CASTLE, Cardigan (SN 164 464). On a promontory 1.5km downstream from the town is a ringwork and bailey that may be 'Geraint's fort' (Dingeraint) built by Roger de Montgomery in 1093. When Gilbert fitz Richard invaded Ceredigion in 1110 he re-founded the site, but whether his castle was here or at nearby Cardigan is uncertain.

An area of headland *25m* by *70m* is defended by an almost straight length of bank, fronted by a rock-cut ditch. At the south corner a causeway over the ditch leads to a small and rather feeble bailey.

80 PANTGLAS (SN 422 260). The tip of a wooded ridge above the Gwili valley is cut off by a short, massive bank up to 6.8m high, with a deep ditch in front. There is a levelled platform about 6m square behind the rampart, but the rest of the enclosure is sloping and unsuited to buildings. Possibly an unusual form of ringwork, or an unfinished Iron Age fort.

81 PARC-Y-CASTELL (SN 288 427)*. A very dubious site. Although marked on OS maps, all that can be seen is a low ridge beside a stream, with a shallow and vague ditch curving around the landward approach. This ditch could be just a natural feature, or else the site may represent a motte that was started, but never finished.

82 PARC-Y-CASTELL, St Davids (SM 744 252)*. This fine example of a partial ringwork lies on the edge of the river Alun close to the cathedral, beside the road to Porth Clais. A massive overgrown bank with an outer ditch curves around a courtyard 27m by 33m, which is defended on the open side by natural slopes. These slopes also protect one flank of an adjoining rectangular bailey. There are faint traces of a worn-down enclosure on the opposite side of the ring, but this might just be an old field boundary.

The castle has no recorded history, but it must have been built by the bishops to protect the early cathedral precinct from attack. A likely period for its construction would be around 1115, when the last native bishop was replaced by a Norman one. John Leland visited Wales in the 1530s and mentioned that there *'remayne tokins of Cairboias Castel standing by Alen Ryvert about a Quarter of a Myle lower than S.David'*.

83 PARC-Y-MARL (SN 047 245). On a hilltop east of Llys-y-fran reservoir is a poorly preserved enclosure about *60m* across, possibly the remains of a ringwork, or an Iron Age fort.

84 PENCADER (SN 444 362)*. According to Gerald of Wales, an old man of Pencader warned Henry II that the Welsh would never be subdued by the wrath of man, unless the wrath of God concurred. The village has no inspiring castle ruin to epitomise this testament of Welsh resistance, but there is a fine motte behind the old school. A wide ditch encircles the landward side of the 5m high mound, which has a broad, level summit 24m across. The only place for a bailey is on the north flank, but the school occupies most of this ridge and the few remaining earthworks look like natural features. This may have been the castle 'in Mabudrud' built by Gilbert de Clare in 1145.

Pencader motte.

85 PENCASTELL (SN 402 379), Castell Mair. In a field opposite St Mary's church is an overgrown motte *6.1m* high and about *18m* across, which has been damaged on one side by a path. The mound is still encircled by a boggy ditch, but there is no sign of an

38

adjoining bailey. However, at the end of the seventeenth century, Edward Llwyd wrote that '*the outworks are defaced, and very near made level by frequent ploweings*'. Other solitary mottes may similarly have lost their baileys to the plough.

86 PENGAWSAI (SN 110 280), Castell Blaenllechog.

This small ringwork lies on enclosed farmland in the foothills of the Preseli Mountains. The ditch has almost vanished, but the remainder of the defences are well-preserved and consist of a rampart up to 3.2m high, enclosing a tiny courtyard

Pengawsai: This tiny ringwork could only have accommodated a little wooden hall or tower (as shown).

10m by 8m. There could only have been room within for a little building or a free-standing wooden tower. A gap in the east bank may mark the entrance.

87 PENYCASTELL (SN 663 675)*.

A small earthwork on the end of a moorland ridge, possibly an unfinished motte. The defensive bank is prominent on the naturally strong north flank, but virtually absent on the remaining sides.

88 PEN-YR-ALLT (SN 158 420).

Several years ago Castell Pen-yr-allt was badly damaged by the landowner, who filled in part of the ditch and flattened a section of the rampart. It lies on a ridge beyond Llantood church and was a large and strong ringwork, possibly with masonry defences.

The internal area measures 40m-44m across, and was enclosed on the weaker sides by a curving stony rampart fronted by a rock-cut ditch over 2m deep. Where best preserved, the bank rises 5.7m above the boggy ditch, but would no doubt have been much higher on the destroyed flank. The remaining sides have been quarried back to form near-vertical cliffs 6m high.

The bank and ditch defences of Pengawsai.

Within the courtyard, a motte-like heap of rubble is thought to mark the remains of a tower. However, the mound shows few signs of solid masonry, just earth and stones, and excavation would really be needed to recover the plan.

89 PICTON (SN 016 135)*, The Belvedere. In woods east of Picton Castle is a densely overgrown mound about *7m* high with an oval summit up to *24m* across. This is believed to be a large motte, and the possible forerunner of nearby Picton. It has suffered much disturbance, with concrete foundations (of a summerhouse?) on the top, and an ornamental grotto in one side.

90 POINTZ CASTLE (SM 830 237)*. This motte was built in the twelfth century by a tenant of the Bishop of St Davids, namely Punch or Ponce, and was later taken over by the clergy and worked as a farm. Presumably the castle was still occupied and used to defend the estate, though later a stone house was built nearby (demolished in the 1950s). The *'Castrum Poncii'* is an overgrown motte rising from a silted ditch close to the A487.

91 PUNCHESTON (SN 009 298)*, Casmael. The old village school stands within an enclosure on the edge of a steep drop to the river Anghof. Where best preserved, the bank is about 3m high with a central entrance gap, and encloses a larger area than most ringworks, raising the possibility that it may be a hillfort.

92 RUDBAXTON (SM 961 205)*. In a fenced-off enclosure beside the parish church is a damaged and overgrown motte about *4m* high with an uneven summit *12m* across. It was probably built by Alexander Rudebac (c1150-1200), who founded the adjacent village.

93 RUDBAXTON RATH (SM 985 188), Simon's Castle, St Leonard's Rath. Frequent ploughing has all but obliterated the ringwork sheltering inside the massive ramparts of an Iron Age hillfort. Only a slight shelf marks the position of a bank and ditch cutting off a third of the interior. Just outside the entrance St Leonard's well can be seen, but the adjoining chapel has long vanished.

94 ST CLEARS (SN 281 154)*, Banc-y-beili. This is one of the largest and most accessible motte and bailey castles in Dyfed, though its current role as a playground is somewhat demeaning. The first certain reference to St Clears occurs in 1188, when Gerald of Wales mentioned that archers from the castle were ordered to join the Crusades as penance for killing a Welsh youth. But the castle had been built long before that, and the adjoining town and priory had been founded around the middle of the twelfth century.

The castle of 'Ystrad Cyngen', burnt by Lord Rhys in 1153, may be a reference to St Clears, since it lies next to the Cynin river. The year after Gerald's visit, Rhys burnt the castle again, and in 1215 Llywelyn Fawr repeated the destruction. It was rebuilt and remained in use well into the fifteenth century, falling to Owain Glyndŵr in 1405. The motte is 8.4m high with a rounded summit about 11m across. The large adjoining bailey has been extended in recent years by dumping. There is a tradition of buried stonework on the mound (which may explain the uneven summit), but only excavation will reveal the plan.

95 ST ISHMAELS (SM 835 076)*. This was an outlying manor of the barony of Walwyn's Castle, and a motte was built to defend the surrounding land. The shaggy, overgrown mound, *20m* high, lies in a field just north of the village.

96 ST MARY'S MOUND (SN 344 442). This motte lies on enclosed farmland close to the ruined church of Llanfair Treflygen. The encircling ditch is fairly complete although the *5.8m* high mound has been damaged on one side.

97 TALLEY (SN 631 334). Two lakes north of Talley abbey are separated by a wooded bog in which lies an ill-defined mound up to 4m high. The summit is uneven and irregular, and there are only vague traces of a ditch. The mound has been identified as a motte, but it is very shapeless and could be a natural feature.

98 TEMPLE BAR (SN 533 544). A sloping headland between two streams is defended on the vulnerable west side by a strong rampart 4.5m high, with an outer ditch. This may be a partial ringwork, but the large internal area is more typical of Iron Age sites.

99 TEMPLETON (SN 110 116)*, Sentence Castle. The narrow building plots running behind the village street preserve something of the layout of the Medieval settlement, which was evidently connected with the Knights Templar (a band of warrior-monks dedicated to protecting pilgrims in the Holy Land).

The settlement was protected by a small ringwork which is now very overgrown and damaged, but is accessible by a public footpath. A strong rampart between 3.4m and 6m high encloses a small courtyard up to 9m across. The surrounding boggy ditch has been enlarged in recent times. A reference to 'a castle in Arberth' destroyed by the Welsh in 1116 is often assumed to be this site, but there is no supporting evidence (as will be discussed in the entry for Narberth).

100 TOMEN LLANIO (SN 661 579)*. This fine motte lies in a prominent position next to the A485 near Tregaron. The mound rises *5m* above a silted ditch, with natural slopes defending the south flank. The summit is *17m* across, and has been dug into on one side. Aside from the dubious Llwyn-gwinau, this is the only castle in Pennardd commote, and is probably the 'castle of Richard de la Mare' burnt in 1136.

101 TOMENLAWDDOG (SN 360 362)*. Beside Penboyr church is a gorse-covered motte 5.8m high, with a silted ditch. Frequent ploughing has obliterated the bailey noted by the RCAHM in 1917. Further damage has been caused by quarrying, revealing the mound to be composed of large blocks of shale rubble.

102 TOMEN RHYD-OWEN (SN 444 447). This motte lies in the Clettwr valley not far from Castell Humfrey, and may also be a relic of the fitz Richard invasion of 1110. The mound is between *3m* and *5.4m* high, with a ditch and counterscarp, and lies on a ridge above the river. The whole site is now very overgrown.

103 TOMENSEBA (SN 325 370)*, Bwlch-y-domen. Like Tomenlawddog a few kilometres away, this motte was built to control the hill country between the Teifi and Tywi valleys, and its remote setting hints at a Welsh origin. The mound is over 6m high with a disturbed summit 16m across. The RCAHM mentions that an early dig uncovered masonry, but this might have been just the stony core of the mound. The surrounding ditch is still a boggy obstacle.

104 TREFILAN (SN 549 571)*. Maelgwn ap Rhys built this large motte before his death in 1231, but it wasn't completed until two years later by his son. The castle remained in Welsh hands until the late thirteenth century, and it may have been the 'house' that King Edward's army burnt in 1282. Maelgwn's castle is a substantial tree-covered mound 8.9m high, encircled by a broad, boggy ditch. Stone foundations noted on the summit in the 1950s can no longer be seen.

105 WALWYN'S CASTLE (SM 873 030)*. This was the stronghold and administrative centre of a large barony occupying much of the St Bride's peninsula, with subordinate castles at Dale and St Ishmaels. By the mid-thirteenth century the estate had been acquired by the de Brian family of Devon, but unlike their main seat at Laugharne, Walwyn's Castle appears to have remained a modest earth and timber fort throughout its existence.

The castle lies on a ridge between two valleys, beside the parish church. The huge earthworks visible today are part of an Iron Age hillfort, and the Normans simply piled up earth behind an inner rampart to form a makeshift motte about 6m high and 18m across. The inconveniently large inner enclosure was subdivided by a slighter bank and ditch to form a narrow bailey. There is much loose stone on top of the motte, and so perhaps there was some form of masonry work here.

106 WAUN-DDU (SN 820 310)*. At more than 360m above sea level, this remote site could only have been a temporary outpost to guard the lonely mountain road from Llandovery to the Usk valley. If it is a genuine motte, then it is probably the smallest in Wales, rising only 1m to an oval summit 18m across. The lofty setting made a high mound unnecessary, and the builders constructed it on the corner of a long disused Roman camp, which was then utilised as a bailey. The camp is about 35m square and defended by a low bank and outer ditch, and it would have been constructed as a field exercise by Roman troops stationed at a nearby fort.

107 WAUN TWMPATH (SN 466 026)*. This overgrown motte lies in an unstrategic position on sloping ground below the crest of a hill. The encircling ditch and counterscarp is well preserved, and the motte stands up to 8m high.

108 WOLF'S CASTLE (SM 957 265)*. The placename *Castrum Lupi* occurs in 1229, but this motte and bailey was certainly built long before that date. A further reference in the Black Book of St Davids (1326) to certain buildings here belonging to the lord of the manor, might imply that the castle was still in use. The tree-covered earthworks can be seen on a ridge beside the A40, and consist of a damaged motte 6m high, with an uneven summit 15.2m across. A small oval bailey occupies the remainder of the steep promontory site.

109 & 110 YSTRADMEURIG*. Gilbert fitz Richard established this important castle in the commote of Mefenydd around 1110. It was burnt by Cadwaladr and Owain Gwynedd in 1137, and in 1151 the young princes of Deheubarth ousted the north Walians and rebuilt the castle. Seven years later the Normans were back in control when Roger de Clare captured his grandfather's stronghold, but it may have been among the castles destroyed by Lord Rhys a few months later.

Rhys must have rebuilt Ystradmeurig, for it changed hands frequently in the dynastic struggles at the close of his reign. Maelgwn besieged and captured it on Christmas Eve 1193, but handed it over to his hated brother Gruffudd in return for some hostages. Maelgwn regained the castle in 1198, but was forced to destroy it in 1208 when his enemy, Llywelyn Fawr, attempted to invade Ceredigion. This drastic policy failed, for Llywelyn still ousted Maelgwn and handed his lands over to the heirs of the deceased Gruffudd. Ystradmeurig is not mentioned again, but, considering its strategic importance, it could hardly have been abandoned so early. More likely is that the subsequent history was never eventful enough to warrant an entry in the Chronicles.

There are two castles at Ystradmeurig and it is not certain which are referred to in the Chronicles. Gilbert's castle was probably the small, but well-preserved motte on the banks of the river Meurig, about 1.5km east of the village (SN 718 677). This is a typical twelfth century mound, rising 4.7m above a silted ditch to a flat summit 13m across.

Exactly when this was replaced by a larger enclosure behind the village (SN 703 676) is not known, but it was probably before 1193 because Maelgwn's attack involved the use of siege machines, which would hardly be needed for a small motte. This second site is a large oval earthwork about *91m* by *116m*, defended on the north and west sides by a rampart and outer ditch. Within this is a smaller enclosure, which could be interpreted as the remains of an earlier ringwork. The

Motte at Ystradmeurig.

robbed foundations of a square stone tower can be seen in the outer enclosure.

111 YSTRAD PEITHYLL (SN 653 824)*.

This remote motte was built by Razo, steward to Gilbert fitz Richard, and is first mentioned in 1116 when it was attacked by Gruffudd ap Rhys. The *Brut* relates how the little castle was burnt by night and the garrison slain. The following day the Welsh army moved on to Aberystwyth, but Razo managed to get help from Earl Gilbert at Ystradmeurig, and the resultant battle is vividly described in the *Brut*. We can assume that Razo was satisfied with his revenge, but the castle makes no further appearance in the Chronicles, and its subsequent history is unknown. The motte is *5m* high with a disturbed summit *10m* across, and lies in the fork of two streams. A well-preserved ditch surrounds the mound except for the north-west flank.

112 YSTUM ENLLI (SN 585 032)*. An

intriguing dual site located within an S-bend of the river Loughor. On the west edge of a low ridge is a 7m high motte with a summit 9-11m across, and a well-marked muddy ditch. The RCAHM mentions the discovery of three swords and masonry remains here c1870, but the existing rubble scattered about could have come from the core of the mound.

About 100m away on the opposite side of the ridge is a very overgrown bank and ditch enclosure about *30m* by *40m* overall. The ditch has mostly been filled in and is absent on the side facing the river. A prominent dip in the middle of the rampart may be the site of an entrance. Earlier accounts have classed this as a moated site, but it is almost certainly a ringwork (albeit of a squarer plan than usual).

There is no recorded history about the site, and the relationship between the motte and the ringwork is unknown. They are unlikely to be contemporary, but which came first? And were they occupied together? On the opposite side of the river is the better-documented motte and bailey of Hugh de Meules, burned by the Welsh in 1215. Evidently, this ancient crossing point between Carmarthenshire and Glamorgan was considered important enough to warrant several fortifications.

ABEREINION was built by Lord Rhys in 1169 and rebuilt by Maelgwn in 1206, but no satisfactory location has been identified. An Abereinion near Llandysul has been suggested, and there are antiquarian references to a motte, but nothing survives today. This could be another name for the motte at Domen Las.

CENARTH BYCHAN was built by Gerald de Windsor in 1108 and evidently lay near Cenarth in the cantref of Emlyn. Cilgerran is the traditional choice.

DINWEILER. An important castle (or place) which appears several times in the Chronicles, and is sometimes confused with Dinefwr. It is first mentioned in 1146 and was built by Gilbert de Clare. Could it have been the unnamed castle in Mabudrud Gilbert had built the previous year? Maredudd and Rhys ap Gruffudd rebuilt Dinweiler (or Dinefwr?) in 1151, and in 1159 a Norman army encamped there (and *measured out a castle* according to one version of the *Brut*). Since the opposing Welsh force was stationed at a place identified as Mynydd Llanybydder, then Dinweiler was presumably close by, making it likely to have been one of the six castles in Mabudrud (perhaps Pencader?). Another theory favours the large motte and bailey at Allt-y-ferin.

GARTH GRUGYN was built by Maelgwn Fychan in 1242, and may have been the unusual earthwork at Llanilar, which lies near the township of Crugyn.

LAMPETER. Samuel Meyrick noted a motte near the parish church (now destroyed), which he conjectured was the original Welsh castle of the district.

LUCHEWEIN was captured by Rhys Gryg in 1206 and 1209, and the similarity of the placename to Llyn Llech Owain suggests it might have been the lost mound at Castell-y-rhingyll nearby.

NANT YR ARIAN. An unlocated Welsh castle mentioned only in 1213. Presumably it lay in the Melindwr valley east of Aberystwyth, and could have been a mound (motte?) near Old Goginan dug away in c1840.

MABUDRUD is the name of a commote and also a castle built by Gilbert de Clare in 1145. There are six sites here, and the large motte at Pencader is a likely choice (see also Dinweiler).

MABWYNION is also a commote, and the castle was captured by the Welsh in 1164. There are only two sites here, Lampeter and Temple Bar, and the former is the probable candidate.

PENBEILI is the suggestive name of a farm near Llangynllo, where a 'tumulus' (a motte?) once existed.

PENWEDDIG is a cantref in north Ceredigion, and also the name of a castle built by the English in 1114. It is probably the earliest reference to Castell Gwallter.

RHYDYGORS. The forerunner to Carmarthen castle built in 1093. It is believed to have stood 1km downstream, and was destroyed when the railway was built in the nineteenth century.

RICHARD'S CASTLE. Destroyed by the Welsh in 1136 along with Aberystwyth and Dinerth. Tomen Llanio is situated between these two places and is the most likely site.

REJECTED SITES.

BEILI-BEDW (SN 738 231). Natural mound.

BRYN MAEN CAERAU (SN 597 483). Natural mound.

CASTELL BUGAD (SN 592 483). Natural outcrop.

CASTELL ELY (SN 193 105). Prehistoric burial mound.

CASTELL Y FRAN (SN 080 222). Prehistoric burial mound.

CRUGYN DIMAI (SN 592 787). Natural outcrop.

PANT Y CADNO (SN 114 225). Natural outcrop, possibly shaped into a feeble motte.

TWRLA (SN 645 369). Old quarry site and mounds.

Stone Castles

Although earth and timber castles were cheap and relatively quick to erect, they had one major disadvantage – vulnerability to fire. The rebuilding of defences in stone was therefore a necessary measure to ensure the long-term survival of a castle, but it was usually carried out in piecemeal fashion when the owner had enough funds available, and during a prolonged period of peace. The present day appearance of a castle can be

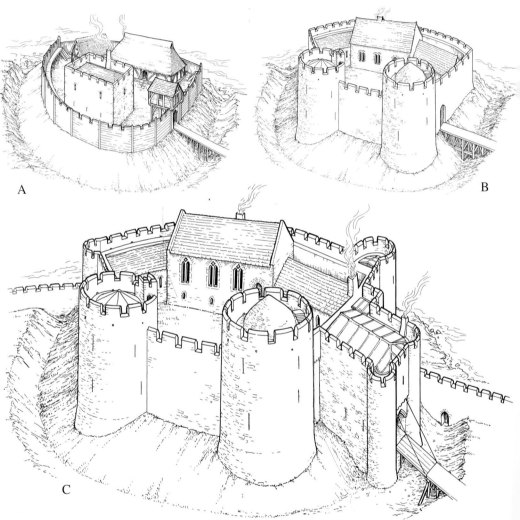

A

B

C

Most castles developed and grew over many years. The reconstructions of Laugharne castle show the Norman ringwork at the end of the twelfth century, with a stone hall or keep within the earlier timber defences (A). By the middle of the thirteenth century stone walls had been added, with a simple gateway, and two large round towers (B). At the end of the century the castle was strengthened and a new gatehouse built (C). Further works were carried out in the fourteenth and sixteenth centuries, resulting in a complex and substantial edifice (see drawing on page 86).

the result of many phases of building over several generations (Carew, Laugharne and Pembroke, for example), or just the work of a comparatively short period (Aberystwyth, Carreg Cennen).

Even in stone castles, timber had an important role to play. Apart from doors, windows, floors and roofs, many of the internal buildings would have been wholly, or partly, built from wood. Temporary defence works such as a brattice or **hourd** (a covered fighting gallery projecting beyond the wall tops) was also timber-framed and could be set up in times of emergency.

The twelfth century witnessed a remarkable surge of building across the country, as the old wooden keeps were transformed into towering structures of stone and mortar. In England, keeps of a square and rectangular plan proliferated in the reigns of Henry I and Henry II, but in the more volatile areas of Wales they tend to be smaller in size and later in date. The keep remained the principal defensive feature of most castles well into the thirteenth century, even when more effective methods of fortification had been developed.

The first record of a stone building in west Wales occurs in 1108, when Gerald de Windsor built *'a wall and a ditch'* at Cenarth Bychan. This unlocated site has traditionally been identified as Cilgerran, and fragments of early masonry survive beneath the thirteenth century structure. Rocky sites like Cilgerran and Pembroke would have provided abundant materials for simple masonry defences, but beyond conjecture we have no definite evidence to prove their existence.

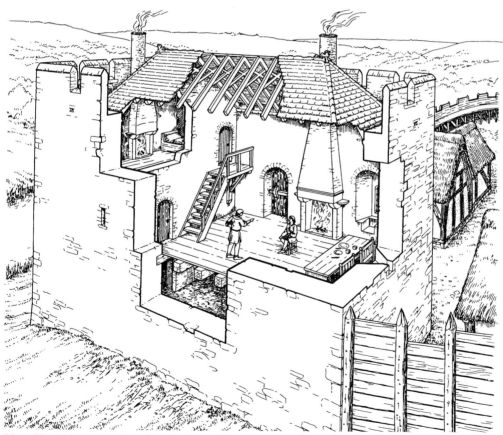

Manorbier: A cutaway view through the twelfth century hall block, showing the relatively comfortable main chamber on the first floor above dark storerooms, with a solar at second floor level.

We must turn further south, to the securely held Anglo-Norman lands of southern Pembrokeshire, to find the earliest substantial remains of a stone castle. At Manorbier, William de Barri constructed a two storeyed hall block within the courtyard of what must have been a partial ringwork. The simple architectural details suggest a date in the second quarter of the twelfth century. The rest of the defences were probably of wood, though a near-contemporary stone tower stood guard beside the gate.

A fragment of Norman stonework discovered at Kidwelly suggests that the de Londres family had a masonry building within the ringwork, and the Old Hall at Pembroke was probably built by Richard de Clare (d.1176). Documentary evidence suggests that there was some form of stone defence on the motte at Llandovery by c1162, and recent excavations at Laugharne uncovered footings of a curtain wall and hall block beneath the remains of the later castle. The Lord Rhys rebuilt Cardigan in 1176, but unfortunately none of his work can be identified with any certainty. Fragments of a late twelfth century keep remain at Haverfordwest, while a small tower at Nevern could be Welsh work of the 1190s. Undateable vestiges of stone towers survive at the earthwork sites of Pen-yr-allt, Eglwyswrw and Ystradmeurig, while Castell Crychydd, Dyffryn-mawr and Llansteffan have remnants of simple curtain walls around the ramparts.

In the closing years of the twelfth century the infiltration of continental ideas began to influence castle design in Britain. The most important and far-reaching of these innovations was the use of rounded mural towers. With square or obtuse angled buildings, the corners created a blind spot for the defenders, and provided any enemy with an ideal target for undermining; the round tower did away with these problems. Furthermore, if the tower was built projecting out from the castle and was provided with strategically placed arrowslits, then archers could cover the ground immediately in front of the walls.

The huge keep at Pembroke castle was one of the first to be built to a round plan in Britain, and its construction was ordered by one of the greatest knights of the Middle Ages, William Marshal (c1146-1219). In 1189 Marshal, a *'landless man with naught but his knighthood'* as one contemporary chronicler described him, married the heiress of Richard de Clare and at a stroke acquired vast estates in Britain and Ireland. Marshal's prowess and chivalrous nature was renowned, and, following the death of King John, he became one of the most powerful men in the land, as regent to the young Henry III. On acquiring the extensive de Clare territories, the earl was in a position to embark on a rebuilding programme at his major strongholds, putting into use the ideas he had undoubtedly picked up on his sojourns in Angevin France.

The tomb effigy of William Marshal, Earl of Pembroke, at the Temple Church, London.

On his return to England in 1204, Marshal began work on rebuilding Pembroke as a power base for his new lordship, and also to serve as a prestigious embarkation point for the Anglo-Norman invasion of Ireland. The round keep has an internal diameter of 7.7m and contains four floors under a vaulted roof crowned with three levels of battlements. The courtyard was enclosed by a strong curtain wall, and entered through a boldly projecting D-shaped gatehouse.

Marshal's son and heir, another William (d.1231), built two similar, though smaller round towers at Cilgerran, which are integrated into the defensive circuit in the manner of normal flanking towers. Guy de Brian IV (d.c1268) was evidently impressed with William's work, for he rebuilt his own castle at Laugharne along similar lines. The foundations of more modest round towers can be seen at Llansteffan, Llawhaden and Nevern, and also at the native strongholds of Dinefwr and Dryslwyn. The stunted keep at Dinefwr, in particular, has features linking it to the towers at Bronllys, Skenfrith and Tretower further east, which have been dated to the period 1210-40. The scant remains at Narberth suggest the keep there belongs to the same group and period, though it differs in having a square flanking tower, known as a **forebuilding**, containing a defended entry.

Gradually the concept of the keep as a solitary (and static) strong point was abandoned in favour of a more integrated defensive circuit, comprising high walls linked to numerous flanking towers. Early experiments were carried out by Hubert de Burgh at Skenfrith and Grosmont (Monmouthshire) in the period 1219-32, and by Ranulph de Blundeville at Beeston (Cheshire) around 1225-32. The Marshal heirs also carried out extensive works at Chepstow and Usk, and were probably responsible for building the outer ward at Pembroke.

By the second half of the thirteenth century any castle of strength could boast at least one line of defence with round towers on the vulnerable angles. The entrance had always been the weakest part of the circuit, and considerable ingenuity was expended on allowing friends in, but keeping foes out. Drawbridges, portcullises, strong wooden doors with drawbars, 'murder holes' in the ceilings to drop rocks on unwelcome heads – all served to defend the gateway. Additional outworks or **barbicans** were built to further increase the hazards facing any attacker, and a particularly good example survives at Tenby.

Early thirteenth century round keeps at Pembroke (left) and Bronllys (right).

Kidwelly: This cutaway reconstruction of the outer gatehouse shows the complex of rooms, stairs, and passageways within the building. The various defensive features include a drawbridge, portcullis and murder holes. The circular opening in the floor of the right-hand room leads to a vaulted dungeon.

50

Early gatehouses tend to be simple rectangular towers with relatively few defensive features, which can be seen at Carew, Manorbier and Tenby; but from the middle of the century the design was perfected by having two towers (usually D-shaped in plan) astride the entrance passage. Guard chambers lay on either side of the heavily defended passageway, and the upper floors were usually large and well-appointed residential chambers. In many cases the gatehouse replaced the keep as the strongest part of the castle. One of the first of this kind was built by Hubert de Burgh for the king at Montgomery (Powys) around 1224-35. Later examples can be seen at Carmarthen, Carreg Cennen, Llansteffan, Llawhaden and Newcastle Emlyn, and the huge, complex structure at Kidwelly is the most ambitious in Dyfed.

In the third quarter of the century, King Edward I continued his campaign to crush Welsh independence, and ordered the building of a string of large castles in mid and north Wales. Some of the new buildings had **concentric** plans, one line of defence within another. The idea was that any invader who had broken through the outer cordon would be faced with a second, more formidable, barrier to cross. There is only one true concentric castle in west Wales – Aberystwyth – which dates from Edward's initial advance against Llywelyn in 1277. However, Kidwelly is in part concentric due to piecemeal construction, and at Carreg Cennen the architect made a noble, but doomed, attempt to impose a rigid plan on an irregular outcrop of rock.

A characteristic feature of these later castles is the use of rounded or hexagonal towers rising from massive, squared bases, with the angles carried up the sides of the tower as pyramidal **spurs**. This greatly strengthened the foundations and hampered any attempt at undermining or battering the walls. Another late refinement was the construction of **machicolations**, where part of the battlements (usually over the gate) was carried forward on projecting **corbels** (stone brackets). A gap in the floor allowed rocks and other missiles to be dropped on enemy heads.

Carreg Cennen castle.

Rebuilding work on the large castles continued well into the fourteenth century, long after there was a need for such fortifications to quell a native uprising. It was not until the beginning of the fifteenth century that English rule was challenged in Wales, and the castles damaged in Glyndŵr's revolt were repaired afterwards. From here on the castle was used as a fortified home, and more money was spent on improving the domestic accommodation rather than strengthening the defences.

Sir Rhys ap Thomas (1449-1525) certainly had the cash and initiative to improve the old strongholds for use in the changing society of the late fifteenth century. Rhys was the grandson of Gruffudd ap Nicholas, and one of the Welsh magnates who rose to power during the reign of Henry VII. At several of his castles Rhys embarked on various

The three raven crest of Sir Rhys ap Thomas, drawn from a tile in Carew church.

building works, and in particular at Carew, he spent large sums of money converting the gloomy Medieval fortress into a Tudor palace. The Elizabethan gentry were no less enthusiastic at building extravagant mansions or enlarging existing ones, and a later owner of Carew, Sir John Perrot (1530-92), added a remarkable north range with an immense long gallery on the top floor. Perrot also modified Laugharne considerably, but any chance these two splendid buildings had of surviving into the present day as 'stately homes', was scuppered in the Civil War.

By the seventeenth century the Medieval castle was hopelessly outdated for military purposes, and although many of the stout walls held back the guns for a while, the end was inevitable. The majority of castles that had been brought back into service were deliberately demolished and left to crumble into picturesque ruin.

The Elizabethan elegance of Sir John Perrot's wing at Carew.

A few castles were lived in more or less continuously, but they needed extensive refurbishment to make them acceptable to the needs of a more sophisticated lifestyle. The process has continued into comparatively recent times, with mansions being built on, or incorporating, ancient remains. Although there are no exuberant Victorian fantasies in west Wales to compare with Penrhyn, Bodelwyddan or Castell Coch, elsewhere in the country, at Newport, Picton and Roch, we can see the final devolution of these ancient strongholds – converted into the needs of a somewhat more civilised age.

BEHIND THE BATTLEMENTS.

Contrary to the image perpetuated by film and TV, life for the average person in the Middle Ages was basic, brutish and short.

The most simple amenities we now take for granted (such as good health, hygiene and privacy) were practically nonexistent. Within the high stone walls of the castle the arrangement of the various rooms was much as it would have been in a normal upper class manor house. Most buildings were two storeyed, with the more important rooms located on the upper floor for security reasons. Ground level rooms were generally used for stores, and in west Wales the roofs of such chambers were usually vaulted in stone to reduce the risk of fire. All the wall-walks, towers, and rooms were linked by stairways formed of stone steps rising in a spiral around a central post or **newel**. Sometimes the stair would be in a straight flight within the thickness of the walls (**intra mural**).

The social heart of the castle was the great hall, a large, barn-like building where all the day-to-day functions, such as administration work, feasting, and (for servants) sleeping, went on. Halls were arranged on a strict hierarchical order; the room was entered at the 'lower' end along a passageway sometimes divided off from the main area by a timber screen. On one side lay storerooms, and beyond the screen stretched the great space of the hall itself. At the far end stood the high table where the lord of the castle and his family sat at meal times. Doors beyond gave access to the private room, or **solar**.

The lofty roof over the hall space may have been steeply pitched and supported by great timber trusses (as at Kidwelly), or covered by a flat wooden ceiling resting on carved beams (Carew, Pembroke). The form of the roof can usually be deduced from details such as corbels, beam holes, and the pitch of surviving gables. The hall was usually heated by an open hearth set on the floor, and the smoke would escape through a louvre or vent in the roof above. Sometimes there was a large wall fireplace, though usually this was reserved for smaller

Present day view of the Great Hall, Pembroke, with a reconstruction drawing showing how the building may have looked in the early fourteenth century. The hall stood over a dark store and kitchen, and the bare walls were probably painted with various designs.

Finely decorated Tudor fireplace at Carew.

chambers which did not have the necessary headroom for the smoke to rise. Good examples of such fireplaces can be seen in the solars at Carew, Kidwelly, Llansteffan and Manorbier.

The other important facility which taxed the Medieval architect's ingenuity was sanitation, and a privy, or **garderobe**, was considered a necessary adjunct to a well-appointed residential chamber. Medieval toilets were based on what Wynford Vaughan-Thomas aptly described as the 'long drop system'. They were little rooms in the thickness of the wall, with a shaft descending to a drain or pit at the bottom. When Owain ap Cadwgan attacked Cenarth Bychan in 1108, the castellan, Gerald de Windsor, had to make an undignified escape through the garderobe drains! Other garderobes were built projecting out from the walls and supported on large stone corbels; good examples of this type can be seen on the battlements at Dinefwr and the town walls at Tenby. A more elaborate step was to have privies on several levels in a tower jutting out beyond the walls (as at Manorbier).

Aside from the hall and solar, the next most important room in the castle was the chapel, and it must be remembered that the Normans were deeply religious (as well as avaricious and cruel). Liturgical consider-

The chapel tower, Kidwelly.

54

ations demanded that the altar faced east, and so the chapel was set as near as possible in this orientation. At Cilgerran the chapel lay on the top floor of the gatehouse, and at Carreg Cennen and Narberth it was housed in a flanking tower. Carew and Kidwelly have very fine purpose-built chapel towers of hexagonal plan, with living quarters for resident priests. Perhaps the most impressive of all is the chapel block at Manorbier, with its vaulted roof and finely carved stonework.

The present day appearance of a castle should not mislead one into thinking that the interiors were dark and grim cells. Walls were generally plastered and whitewashed, and the more important rooms would

Early thirteenth century unglazed window at Cilgerran.

probably have had painted decorations. Panelling and wainscoting were common in the later Middle Ages, and rush-strewn floors gave way to gleaming tiles. Glass, however, was an expensive commodity. Most windows were just unglazed openings in the walls, closed by shutters to control draughts. Windows were of two types; narrow splayed loopholes for archers to use, and other, wider openings for light and ventilation (but always barred to prevent a break-in).

The form of window and door heads can be vital in determining the age of a building. Norman architecture is characterised by the use of simple, rounded arches, and can be found in buildings from the eleventh to the early thirteenth centuries (Cilgerran, Manorbier, Pembroke). Pointed arches and those with cusped heads belong to the thirteenth and fourteenth centuries, and the more elaborate the stonework, the higher the status of the building it adorns. Finally, the fifteenth and early sixteenth century Perpendicular style is typified by plainer windows and doors with a distinctive flattened 'Tudor' arch (Carew). Small square headed windows have a broad date range, but those found in large panels are Elizabethan, and occur principally at Carew and Laugharne.

Gazetteer.

Unless otherwise stated, all the castles in the following section are accessible to the public, and are prominently situated in towns and villages. Most have signposted directions from the nearest main road. Of these sites, Benton, Cardigan and Newport are privately owned and not normally accessible. There is limited access to Dinefwr while restoration work proceeds, and Picton is only open on certain days in the summer.

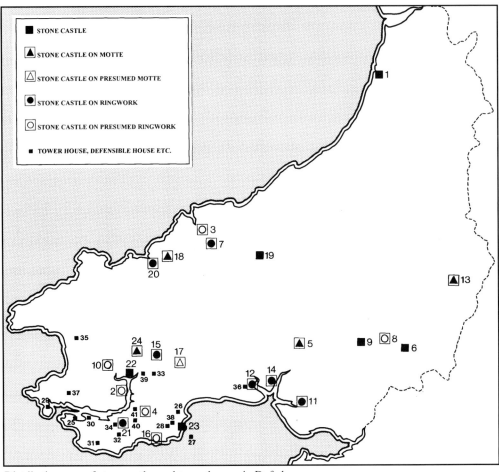

Distribution map of stone castles and tower-houses in Dyfed.

STONE CASTLES

1	Aberystwyth	13	Llandovery
2	Benton	14	Llansteffan
3	Cardigan	15	Llawhaden
4	Carew	16	Manorbier
5	Carmarthen	17	Narberth
6	Carreg Cennen	18	Nevern
7	Cilgerran	19	Newcastle Emlyn
8	Dinefwr	20	Newport
9	Dryslwyn	21	Pembroke
10	Haverfordwest	22	Picton
11	Kidwelly	23	Tenby
12	Laugharne	24	Wiston

TOWER HOUSES, FORTIFIED MANORS etc.

25	Angle	34	Priory Farm
26	Bonville's Court	35	Roch Castle
27	Caldey Priory	36	Roche Castle
28	Carswell & West Tarr	37	Sandyhaven
29	Dale	38	Scotsborough House
30	Eastington	39	Sister's House
31	Flimston	40	Upper Lamphey Farm
32	Kingston Farm	41	Upton Castle
33	Newhouse		

ABERYSTWYTH (SN 579 816)

History. The shattered ruin perched on a headland above the sea is all that remains of a great fortress built in 1277 by Edmund, brother of King Edward I, and the last in a long line of castles stretching back to the early twelfth century. The confusing early history of Aberystwyth has been outlined in the previous section, and although the new foundation of 1277 was built beside the estuary (aber) of the Rheidol, it still retained the name of its predecessor.

The castle was built in the aftermath of the king's first war against Llywelyn, and since it was a royal foundation there exists a good deal of paperwork detailing building costs and repairs. Work began in July, after 240 masons and carpenters were recruited at Bristol. A boundary fence or *bretagium* was first set up to enclose and protect the workings, and for this Edmund ordered more labourers and 6000 nails!

The following year the Earl of Pembroke, William de Valence, was sent to oversee the

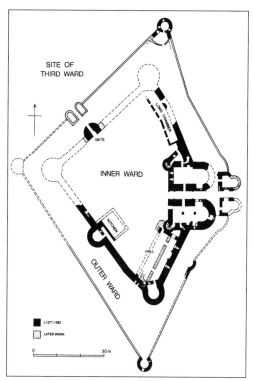

Plan of Aberystwyth castle.

The postern gate, Aberystwyth.

works, and he reported to the king that money had run out due to the large number of workmen employed. The situation was remedied and money was sent. However, when Bevis de Knoville was appointed keeper in 1280, he claimed that the castle was without arms, garrison or provisions, and that the town gates were unlocked and the walls unfinished. Bevis criticised the existing work and said that the gatehouse was shaken by the crash of the waves, having been constructed too close to the ditch. He urgently requested the presence of the royal architect, Master James of St George, but as James was busy at Rhuddlan and could not be spared, a Master Thomas was sent instead.

During the next year a mere £12 was spent on the castle, compared with £199 on the walls of the adjoining town. In this unfinished state the castle was captured by the Welsh in the Easter uprising of 1282. It was burnt along with the town, but the soldiers were spared because *'of the imminence of the days of the Passion'*. Later

Aberystwyth: a bird's-eye reconstruction of Edward I's huge coastal fortress, as it might have appeared in the early fourteenth century. The concentric plan (one line of defence within another) is clear in this view. In the foreground the vanished barbican and town walls can be seen.

that year, Master James was sent to help with the rebuilding, and placed the works in charge of an associate, Master Giles. Because of de Knoville's foresight in suggesting the construction of a harbour, Aberystwyth was supplied by sea during another uprising in 1294-5, and endured a prolonged siege. When finally completed the castle had cost around £4000, and was a concentric fortress on the scale of Rhuddlan and Harlech in north Wales.

Aberystwyth castle became the possession of Prince Edward in 1301, but within forty years the great building was in a very poor state; the roofs and timberwork of the internal buildings were in decay, chimneys had been knocked down by the wind, and the walls and turrets of the third ward *'cast down by the force of the sea'*. The crumbling castle was granted by the Black Prince (son of Edward III) to various favourites who cared little for its upkeep.

From 1404 to 1408 Aberystwyth was held by Owain Glyndŵr, and was only recaptured

with the aid of 'the King's gun' – one of the earliest recorded instances of artillery humbling a castle. During the Civil War, however, the guns finished the job off. In 1637 a royal mint was set up within the walls, coining money with silver dug from local mines, but with the outbreak of hostilities the operation was moved to Shrewsbury. After heavy bombardment the Royalist garrison surrendered in 1646, and although the mint was briefly restarted, Parliament gave the order for the demolition of the defences in 1649. The workgangs were so thorough that even today the full ground plan has not been recovered, but excavations have revealed that some of the walls were bonded in clay, rather than mortar, and so shoddy workmanship may account for much of the destruction.

Architecture. The plan, as finally built, comprised two diamond-shaped wards with flanking towers, a barbican, and a third ward on the outer headland (which was destroyed

58

by the sea as early as 1343). The adjoining town was also protected by strong walls with three gates, but all the defences were removed in the nineteenth century. The outer ward has round towers on three of the corners, a twin-towered gatehouse leading to the barbican, and a smaller postern gate providing access to the lost third ward. Much of the surviving masonry is the product of extensive Victorian restoration work.

The massively defended inner ward closely follows the plan of the outer, but the walls were thicker and higher and the corner towers much larger. In addition, the south flank had an extra tower midway along its length. The only part of the castle to survive up to battlement level is the postern gate on the north wall. The principal feature of Aberystwyth castle – indeed of many castles of this period – was the huge inner gatehouse. This had two elongated D-shaped towers on either side of a long entrance passage defended by arrowslits, a portcullis, and three sets of stout wooden doors. All the upper floors have disappeared, but there would have been spacious chambers including the constable's residence, and a room for working the portcullis mechanism. In all likelihood the royal appartments were housed on the uppermost floor.

Surveys carried out in 1320 and 1343 list various buildings within the castle including the kitchen, bakehouse, stable, granary, Long Chamber, and *'the great chamber adjoining the chapel'* – presumably the hall. Recent excavations have uncovered the foundations of some of these buildings, but no doubt more remain to be discovered beneath the grass and rubble.

Refs: HKW / AC 1977 / Ceredigion 1995 / Jones 1977

BENTON (SN 005 068)

History. Situated on a natural outcrop of volcanic rock, Benton rises like 'an ivory tower' from the wooded hillside overlooking the Cleddau river. This is one of the least-known castles in west Wales, and has been a private residence since Ernest Pegge began rebuilding the neglected ruin in the 1930s. Little is known of its history, though it belonged to the barony of Walwyn's Castle, and is thought to have been built by Bishop Thomas Bek (1280-93) of St Davids. Benton was held for a time by the de la Roche family of Roch castle, and later passed briefly to Sir John Perrot.

Architecture. The surviving parts of Benton have been extensively restored and incorporate much modern work, but fortunately the nineteenth century castleologist, G.T.Clark, published a fairly detailed survey of the building in 1865. His account suggests there was an inner courtyard (a ringwork?) enclosed by a curtain wall, with an earthwork outer enclosure that may have been a bailey (though Clark thought it was a 'cattle pound').

The courtyard was entered through a very simple arched gateway (lacking even a portcullis) flanked on one side by a little turret, and on the other by a small, three storeyed round tower. There are no fireplaces or stairs in this tower, and the wooden floors must have been reached by ladders and trapdoors. The presence of a garderobe turret suggests this cramped and primitive tower may have had some residential use, although it is likely that the main accommodation was in the courtyard itself. Clark also noted a more ruined tower on the north side of the inner enclosure.

Today, the restored gateway and round tower survive, but dating evidence is lacking. The most distinctive feature is the octagonal parapet on the round tower, which also appears on the late thirteenth century gatehouse at Newport. However, the simple defences and basic details (particularly the absence of a portcullis) would suggest a date in the early part of the thirteenth century.

Refs: AC 1865 / RCAHM 1925 / Miles / Jones.

CARDIGAN (SN 178 459)

History. Cardigan has much in common with Aberystwyth; both were founded by Gilbert fitz Richard of Clare in 1110; both had a confused early history, and at the two sites there is little left to see. In that year Henry I dispossessed Cadwgan ap Bleddyn of Ceredigion, and granted the land to Gilbert, who then built two castles. One was at Aberystwyth, and the other '*near the estuary of the Teifi, in the place called Dingeraint*'. The Chronicles mention that this place had been fortified by Roger de Montgomery in 1093, but whether this was the site of Cardigan itself, or the ringwork at Old Castle further downstream, is not certain. In any event, Roger's outpost was destroyed in the Welsh uprising of 1094, and it was left to Earl Gilbert to spearhead the second invasion of Ceredigion, using Cardigan as a new base.

Gilbert established a Benedictine priory nearby, and probably also encouraged the development of an adjoining settlement. The princes of Gwynedd failed to dislodge the invaders in 1136 and 1138, but Lord Rhys was more successful in 1165. Five years later Henry II confirmed Rhys as Justiciar of West Wales and allowed him to rebuild the castle, where he held the first recorded Welsh eisteddfod in 1176. '*At Christmas in that year the Lord Rhys ap Gruffudd held court in splendour at Cardigan, in the castle. And he set two kinds of contests there: one between bards and poets, another between harpists . . . and various classes of music craft. And he honoured [the victors] with ample gifts*'.

After Rhys's death the castle was caught up in the rivalry between his squabbling offspring. Maelgwn usurped his brother Gruffudd's right of succession, and in 1198 seized Cardigan and handed over Gruffudd as a prisoner to the English. Gruffudd was soon released, and so the scheming Maelgwn sold '*the lock and stay of all Wales, the castle of Cardigan*' to King John for '*a small worthless price*'. Fifteen years later it was back in Welsh hands, but was surrendered to William Marshal II who arrived from Ireland

with a large fleet. In 1231 Maelgwn Ieuanc laid siege to the castle and breached the walls with the aid of catapults, until the garrison was forced to surrender. By 1240 Cardigan was once more in English control and remained so, apart from a brief tenure by Owain Glyndŵr in 1405.

Edward I made Cardigan the administrative centre for the new shire, and royal accounts provide a detailed survey of the various repairs and building work carried out over the subsequent years. The castle was twice besieged and captured during the Civil War, and a World War II pillbox on the battlements shows that the 'lock and stay of all Wales' still had a role to play in the defence of the country.

Architecture. Despite this long and eventful history, the surviving remains are disappointing to say the least, and the castle has suffered much from post-Medieval neglect and indifference. In 1810 a large house was built on the site, and the courtyard levelled up and turned into an ornamental garden. While the potential for discovering buried features remains high, the pressure on the outer walls has been mounting over the years, so that now only an ugly cradle of metal girders holds the river frontage in place.

We know from documentary evidence that much building work was carried out in the Middle Ages, but identifying the various phases is more problematical. In 1171 Lord Rhys rebuilt the castle '*in stone and mortar*', and repairs were carried out by the English in 1204-5 and 1223. Walter Marshal instigated a rebuilding scheme in 1240 which was continued by his successor, Robert Waleran. Robert received more than £400 to build a keep in 1250, and eleven years later more money was given to complete it up to second floor level. Further repairs were carried out in 1275.

Despite being the royal powerbase for Cardiganshire, the castle was in a poor state by 1343; all the domestic buildings were claimed to be ruined, and the Great Watchtower (probably the keep) was badly decayed. Yet more work was carried out to repair the damage sustained in the Glyndŵr uprising, and a new hall, chamber, and tower were built in 1410; the latter at the sizeable cost of £129. This appears to be the last recorded expenditure on the upkeep, but further consolidation work was carried out periodically, including the building of mock battlements in the 1930s.

Several antiquarian sketches and a survey carried out in 1984 by the Dyfed Archaeological Trust, enable us to conjecture that the castle was a narrow oval enclosure on a rocky bluff above the river. A ditch and counterscarp bank defended the landward flank. There are square bastions on two corners, a rounded turret on the south (visible from Bridge Street), and a projecting D-shaped tower on the east side. This tower contains two stair passages decending to basement garderobes.

On the north side facing the town is a stunted tower of D-shaped plan, rising from a spur base, which has been incorporated into the Georgian house. Only the vaulted basement and part of the upper floor remain, and it is not altogether clear if it was just a flanking tower, or part of the gatehouse. Stylistically it belongs to the late thirteenth or early fourteenth century, and the east tower is possibly contemporary. An engraving of 1741 by the Buck brothers shows this tower with spurs too. An earlier representation of Cardigan by John Speed c1610, shows a highly stylised structure with square (instead of round) towers, and a tall cylindrical keep standing in the courtyard. Speed's drawing also shows the course of the vanished town wall, which had four gateways and at least one flanking tower.

The decaying mansion sits empty now in the overgrown interior of the castle, and the last resident, who for some years used to allow visitors to explore the passages of the east tower armed with a candle, has moved out into a caravan. Every so often plans are announced to try and save the crumbling walls but, at the time of writing, the girders and ivy are still in place.

Refs: HKW / Soulsby / Ceredigion 1985 / Brut

CAREW (SN 045 037)

History. Despite its appearance as an elegant, palatial mansion with rows of spacious mullioned windows, Carew castle was originally a residential fortress; and the military design and function is still visible today, despite extensive alterations in less war-like times. Carew is, in effect, an architectural wolf in sheep's clothing.

According to tradition the constable of Pembroke, Gerald de Windsor, acquired Carew as dowry on his marriage to Nest, the daughter of the late prince Rhys ap Tewdwr. Since the lordship lies so close to the main Norman base at Pembroke it seems highly improbable that the Welsh had any choice in Gerald's acquisition. His descendants styled themselves 'de Carew', and included two Bishops of St Davids, with important branches in Ireland and Somerset. For most of the Medieval period the castle had an uneventful history, though William de Carew apparently offended King John who temporarily seized control of the 'house of carrio' in 1210. Sir Nicholas (d.1311) was responsible for building much of the castle that survives today, and his impressive tomb-effigy can be seen in the nearby parish church, along with floor tiles that bear the three raven crest of Sir Rhys ap Thomas.

Rhys gained the castle through a mortgage arrangement with Sir Edmund Carew around 1480, and proceeded with extensive alterations and restoration work, transforming the grim Medieval fortress into a sumptuous residence. The surviving fragments of carved stonework at the castle testify to the expensive aesthetic tastes of this ambitious magnate. By shrewdly supporting Henry Tudor's claim to the throne against Richard III, Rhys was rewarded with vast estates to add to the family collection. In 1507 he became a Knight of the Garter, and to celebrate the event held a lavish five-day tournament at the castle attended by more than 600 nobles.

This was the high point of Carew's history. Rhys's grandson and heir, Rhys ap Griffith, was unlucky enough to fall foul of

Carew: The Tudor gatehouse to the inner ward. In the background the chapel tower and Sir John Perrot's wing can be seen.

The inner ward, Carew.

the suspicious Henry VIII, and in 1531 he was executed for alleged treason. All his property went to the Crown, but in 1558 Queen Mary granted Carew to Sir John Perrot. He was a scion of a widespread Pembrokeshire family and, if the rumours are true, an illegitimate son of Henry VIII, but his boisterous nature and foul tongue proved to be his undoing. Made Lord Deputy of Ireland in 1584 and then a member of the Privy Council, Perrot was convicted of High Treason in 1591 and sent to the Tower to await execution. Elizabeth seemed reluctant to condemn her half-brother and may have been about to release him, but Perrot died of natural causes and Carew once more passed

to the Crown. Sir John had been engaged in rebuilding Carew and Laugharne, but the works may never have been finished, and subsequent owners of both properties found such enormous Elizabethan schemes too costly and ambitious to maintain. Certainly by 1611 Carew was in an advanced state of decay, and a survey of 1631 mentions rotten beams and fallen roofs. By this time the castle had been regained by the Somerset branch of the Carews, but their tenure of the crumbling edifice did not last long. With the outbreak of civil war Carew was held for the king, but changed hands twice before the Parliamentarian force employed guns to humble the fortress in September 1645.

The great hall at Carew. This reconstruction shows the grand chamber after refurbishment in the late fifteenth century by Sir Rhys ap Thomas. The porch with its coat of arms can be seen, along with the conjectural minstrel's gallery and panelled walls. The figures stand in a great bay window designed to illuminate the high table.

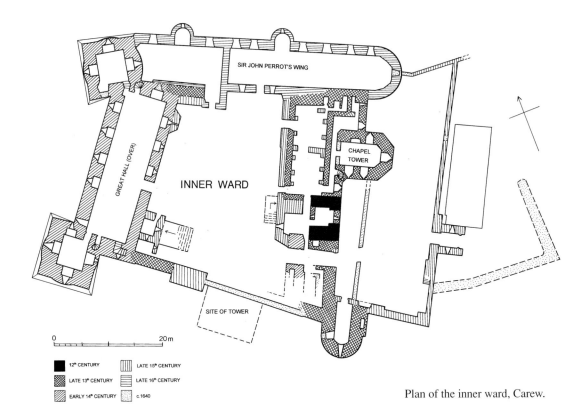

GREAT HALL (OVER)

SIR JOHN PERROT'S WING

INNER WARD

CHAPEL TOWER

SITE OF TOWER

0 ____ 20m

Plan of the inner ward, Carew.

There is some evidence that part of the building was occupied by tenants after the war, but the Carews soon abandoned their ancestral home for the more congenial residence of Crowcombe Court in Somerset.

Architecture. Carew is one of the most complete and best preserved castles in west Wales, and its relatively long life (c1100 – c1650) is commemorated by a wealth of architectural styles and building phases. Little remains of the original castle above ground, but archaeologists have identified a series of rock-cut ditches crossing the neck of the ridge, and which formed the defences of a settlement occupied in the Iron Age, Roman period, and Dark Ages. Perhaps this early fortification was used by Gerald de Windsor as a ready-made ringwork. The Carews were responsible for building some stone defences here – a simple gatehouse of c1200 is walled up in the later buildings – but the bulk of the surviving masonry was raised towards the end of the thirteenth century by Sir Nicholas.

The plan was a rectangular enclosure with flanking towers of various shapes (the inner ward), and a larger, but less heavily defended outer enclosure on the level eastern side.

The castle is approached from the village by a track that passes close to a magnificent tenth century Celtic cross, a memorial to a local Dark Age king. Only a hummocky field marks the site of the outer ward, but recent excavations have revealed the foundations of the Medieval and Tudor defences flattened in the Civil War. As at Manorbier, this missing ward would have doubled the enclosed area of the original castle, and within it stood various buildings including a bakery, brewery, stables and a blacksmith's forge.

The surviving outer gatehouse is a modest Tudor addition, and in front of it is a V-shaped wall built in the Civil War to deflect a direct attack on the entrance. Once through the gate the visitor is confronted by the massive east face of the inner ward, with the polygonal chapel tower on the right and, beyond that, the curved face of Sir John

Perrot's buildings. The whole of this east range is a well-preserved maze of cellars, passages, stairs and apartments, making an exploration of the castle an interesting and exciting experience. The masonry here is extremely complex and embodies work from the twelfth to the seventeenth centuries. All the principal rooms occupy two or three floors above vaulted undercrofts, and include guest chambers, a large dining hall, and accommodation for the resident priest. The chapel has a fine rib-vaulted ceiling with an upper chamber apparently used as a solar – it was certainly a very elegant room, with tiled floors and a richly decorated fireplace. According to tradition Henry VII stayed in the adjoining chamber where there is another fine mantelpiece bearing the royal crest.

Most of the south side of the inner ward was destroyed in the Civil War, but a survey of the confiscated property of Rhys ap Griffith, compiled in 1532, mentions a three storeyed tower midway along the wall. This contained *'a larder house, a kechyn above the same, with half a lofte over and a waye ledyng in to the batilments, and at one corner a little turret'*. A similar turret survives embedded in later masonry on the opposite side of the courtyard.

At the western end of the inner ward lies the great hall, an immense two storeyed building with round towers on the outer corners. Each tower is three storeys high with residential chambers on the upper floors, amply provided with fireplaces, garderobes, and spacious windows. The hall itself was a single long room over a vaulted undercroft, heated by two fireplaces and a central hearth, and illuminated by generous windows. Important guests would have approached this noble building through a Tudor porch proudly displaying the arms of King Henry VII, Prince Arthur, and Catherine of Aragon (who was later to become the bride of Arthur's brother, Henry, after Arthur's unexpectedly early death). Inside, a timber partition separated the entrance passage from the main space of the hall, with a large minstrel's gallery above. Here, during the festivities of 1507, Sir Rhys ap Thomas presided over a great feast *'seasoned with a diversite of musick'*.

The entire north side of the courtyard is occupied by an immense three storeyed wing with rows of mullioned windows and semi-circular bays on each floor. This is the legacy of Sir John Perrot, and it must rank as one of the best examples of Elizabethan architecture in west Wales. The entire top floor was an immense long gallery where Sir John and his guests could stroll in inclement weather, and overlook the surrounding parklands, or admire the paintings and tapestries hung on the wainscotted walls. At least that was the intention; but it is not certain if the building was ever completed before his downfall, and now the great ruin with its empty windows gazes down at the placid waters of the millpond.

Refs: AC 1956 / AJ 1962 / Austin

CARMARTHEN (SN 413 200)

History. When the Normans invaded Dyfed in 1093 they established a number of earthwork castles which were destroyed by the Welsh in the following year, except for Pembroke and Rhydygors. The former is well known, but the site of the latter is uncertain. It probably stood a short distance down-stream from the existing castle of Carmarthen, and was built by William fitz Baldwin. When William died in 1096 the garrison decided to abandon the castle, and it was not until 1105 that Rhydygors was re-occupied, by Richard fitz Baldwin.

Within a few years the castle of Carmarthen (probably not Rhydygors, but a large motte and bailey on the site of the present ruin) had been established as a seat of Royal power, and Henry I allowed trusted Welshmen to hold the castle to prove their allegiance to the Crown. In 1116 Gruffudd ap Rhys launched a surprise attack at night, and

Carmarthen castle gatehouse.

in the confusion the constable, Owain ap Caradog, was killed, although only the '*outer castle*' or bailey was damaged.

In 1137 Cadwaladr and Owain Gwynedd succeeded where Gruffudd failed, and burnt the fortress to the ground. Gilbert de Clare rebuilt it in 1145, but the castle fell to Cadell ap Gruffudd the following year. Cadell later repaired Carmarthen '*for the strength and splendour of his kingdom*'. But the fortunes of war were reversed, and Carmarthen was back in English hands by 1159 when Lord Rhys attacked, but failed to capture it. A large sum of money was spent on repairing the defences and although the castle endured another siege by Rhys, it was destroyed by Llywelyn Fawr in 1215.

When Llywelyn made his peace with Henry III he was granted custody of Carmarthen, but in 1223 William Marshal II broke the treaty and seized Cardigan and Carmarthen from the Welsh, and rebuilt the defences. By 1226 Carmarthen was back in royal control, and King Henry later granted it to Hubert de Burgh, an influential and important figure in the history of castle-building in Wales. However, Hubert's tenure was too short to have influenced the building scheme, and on his fall from royal favour in 1232, the castle passed to Gilbert Marshal.

The following year, Gilbert's elder brother, Richard, turned against Henry and enlisted help among the Welsh leaders to capture and destroy a number of castles in south Wales. Carmarthen held out against a bitter three-month siege, and Richard was forced to depart for Ireland, where he was murdered in 1234. Following Gilbert's death in a tournament in 1241, the castle passed to Robert Waleran, Justiciar of West Wales, and then to Prince Edward in 1254 who later transferred ownership to his brother Edmund. In 1279 Edward, now king, resumed possession in order to make Carmarthen the administrative centre of the newly created shire, and during the next two centuries the building was regularly repaired by appointed chamberlains.

For six years the castle was in the hands of

the Glyndŵr rebels, and a substantial sum was needed to repair the damage caused. The castle was besieged during the Civil War (some of the artillery defences can still be seen west of the town centre) and was then partially demolished by Parliament. What remained was altered and tidied up when the site was used as a county jail in 1789, and then again in 1938 when the existing County Hall was built.

Architecture. As with Cardigan, the varied history of the castle is not reflected in the wealth of visible remains, though here, at least, visitors can walk around the shattered walls. All that remains is the western side of the defences, with three towers and a gatehouse, and it is very difficult to envisage the layout of the rest of the enclosure.

From the various surveys carried out by royal administrators we know that the castle had five towers, a keep (*magna turris*), a hall, chapel, stable, kitchen and gate, and in 1424 one of the buildings is listed as a 'Justice Hall' or courtroom. In recent years the site has been cleaned up and repaired, and some of the dilapidated buildings abutting the old walls have been removed so that more of the castle can be seen. Most obvious of all is the large twin-towered gatehouse in Nott's Square, which was built in the early fifteenth century to replace the gate damaged by Glyndŵr. South of this is a round corner tower with spurs, an addition of c1300, while just to the east of this is a little square building of c1400 known as the Water Tower – either from its proximity to the river, or because it overlooked a postern leading to the quay. Recent works have made the vaulted basements and winding stairs of both towers accessible to the public.

The original motte can still be detected in the form of rising ground behind Queen Street, and if the surviving traces are anything to go by, then it must have been a very large mound – as would befit a royal fortress. On the summit is a walled enclosure of irregular plan, known as a shell-keep. There are rounded bastions on two corners, but most of the visible stonework is modern and overlies the remains of the older wall. The interior is almost completely filled with earth (the remains of the motte?), and recent excavations by the Dyfed Archaeological Trust have revealed the buried footings of a circular stone building on the summit. This has an internal diameter of only 2.9m, and might have been a small and early example of a round keep, or perhaps the foundations of a vanished timber structure. Only large-scale excavation at some future date might unravel the mystery of this curious building. *Refs: Brut / HKW / RCAHM 1914 / Soulsby / DAT.*

CARREG CENNEN (SN 667 192)

History. Legend places the origin of this grim fortress back in the days of King Arthur, but history informs us that Carreg Cennen was a Welsh stronghold of the thirteenth century. Archaeological finds from the vicinity suggest that the rugged limestone

Carreg Cennen: the passage to the cave.

crag on which the castle stands, was inhabited in Iron Age and Roman times. Only in 1248 does Carreg Cennen appear in contemporary records, when Rhys Fychan regained control after his spiteful mother, Matilda de Breos, handed the castle over to the English. Unfortunately, no further details of this salacious family feud are recorded, and the next reference to the site is in 1277, when King Edward I seized the Welsh lands.

The castle was first placed in the control of Payn de Chaworth, lord of Kidwelly, then to the charge of Bevis de Knoville; but with the outbreak of war in 1282 the Welsh were back in occupation. The following year the victorious Edward granted Carreg Cennen to John Giffard, a Gloucestershire knight and loyal servant of the Crown. Giffard briefly lost the castle to Rhys ap Maredudd in 1287, but on its recovery, he set about rebuilding the war-worn fortress on an ambitious scale. During the fourteenth century the property passed through several hands until, in 1340, it was acquired by Henry, Duke of Lancaster. When the duke's

descendant, Henry Bolingbroke, ascended the throne as King Henry IV, Carreg Cennen became Crown property.

During the revolt of Owain Glyndŵr the castle was surrounded by the rebels, and the constable begged Owain in vain to allow his wife and mother-in-law to depart under safe conduct. The fortress was besieged and captured, and the subsequent large sums spent on repairs leaves little doubt that the building was severely damaged. The work had hardly been completed when war broke out again, and the castle was garrisoned by Gruffudd ap Nicholas of Dinefwr, a loyal supporter of the beleaguered King Henry VI. With the Yorkist victory at Mortimers Cross in 1461, the Lancastrian supporters were defeated, and the garrison at Carreg Cennen surrendered. Five hundred workmen spent the following summer rendering the building indefensible, bringing the history of this particular castle to an early end. Henry VII granted the property to Gruffudd's grandson, Sir Rhys ap Thomas, but there is no evidence

Carreg Cennen; the impregnable southern flank.

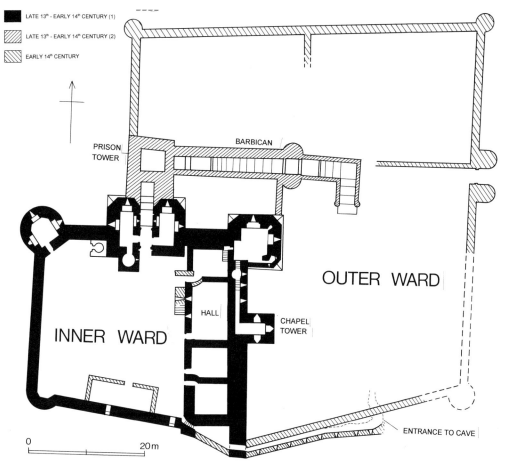

PRISON TOWER

BARBICAN

OUTER WARD

INNER WARD

HALL

CHAPEL TOWER

ENTRANCE TO CAVE

0   20m

Plan of Carreg Cennen.

that Rhys ever bothered to make this remote site habitable again.

Architecture. Of the first Welsh castle here, not a scrap remains, and it would be pointless to speculate on its original appearance. Giffard's fortress was built in three main stages; first the inner ward, then the elaborate barbican defences, finally the outer enclosure. Rock-cut ditches surround the rectangular inner ward on all sides except on the south, where the sheer cliffs gave more than adequate protection. Three flanking towers of a round, square and hexagonal plan were built to defend the more level approaches on the north and east, from where any attack would most obviously be launched. The gatehouse stands between the two larger towers, and although it is badly

ruined now, enough survives to identify it as a typical structure of the Edwardian period. All the residential apartments are set against the east wall and include a kitchen, hall, chamber, and solar, with a little chapel on the top floor of a projecting turret. The second building phase witnessed the construction of a long ramp leading up to the gatehouse. This was elaborately defended by four deep pits crossed by moveable bridges, and a square gatehouse (the Prison Tower). Only a few low foundations survive of the outer ward enclosure, and it was never as strongly defended as the rest of the castle.

Perhaps the most surprising feature of Carreg Cennen is a vaulted passage leading from the courtyard and along the cliff edge, to a cave running deep under the castle. The dark, slippery tunnel ends in a small chamber

Carreg Cennen: A cutaway view through the inner gatehouse, as it would have appeared soon after construction circa 1300. The timber ramp was soon replaced by a more elaborate stone barbican.

with a natural basin fed by water dripping from above. The Tudor antiquarian John Leland even believed that the cave stretched all the way to Worm's Head in Gower! The so-called well has led people to suggest that the cave was blocked up to allow the garrison a safe route to its water supply. But there is an insufficient quantity here, and there are two cisterns in the courtyard designed to catch rainwater for drinking. Part of the cave was used as a dovecot, but it seems most likely that it was sealed to prevent an enemy from being established there.

Refs: Brut / Leland / CADW

CILGERRAN (SN 195 431)

History. This twin-towered castle, beloved of ninteenth century artists and topographers, began existence as a humble earth and timber fort in the Welsh territory of Emlyn. Although Cilgerran is first mentioned in 1165, it must have been founded earlier in the century when the Normans were making inroads into native lands, and could well have been the castle of Cenarth Bychan, built by the constable of Pembroke, Gerald de Windsor, in 1108. Presumably this was another name for the western-most and smaller of the two commotes of Emlyn, and the only other fortification in this land is Castell Crychydd.

In 1165 the castle of Cilgerran was taken by the Lord Rhys, and despite two ineffective sieges the following year, it remained in Welsh

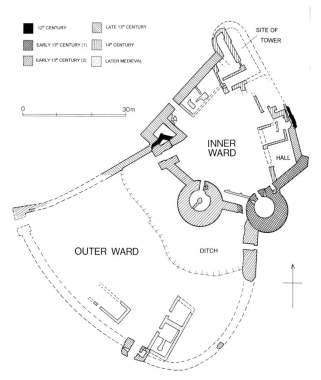

Plan of Cilgerran.

Two round towers guard the inner ward of Cilgerran.

71

Cilgerran: A reconstruction of the inner ward with a cutaway view through one of the two great defensive towers. This drawing shows how Cilgerran may have looked in the late thirteenth century; the plan was altered in the following century by the addition of more domestic buildings and another tower.

hands until 1204. After eleven years the Welsh regained control, but in 1223 the English, led by the Earl of Pembroke, William Marshal II, captured Cilgerran and began to build '*an ornate castle of mortar and stones*'. Cilgerran remained with the Marshals until it passed via an heiress to the Cantelupes of Abergavenny, then to the Hastings family, and finally to the king in the late fourteenth century. The buildings had decayed as early as 1275, and by 1326 the castle was said to be in ruins. The threat of a French invasion prompted Edward III to order many castles, including Cilgerran, to be re-fortified, but it was not until the early fifteenth century that it was subjected to the depredations of warfare and held for a time by Glyndŵr.

Cilgerran castle apparently remained in use as a residence for many years afterwards, and was last inhabited in the sixteenth century by the Vaughan family.

Architecture. The castle lies on a rocky promontory above the river Teifi, with the natural slopes providing excellent defence on all but the southern approach. The defences were therefore massed on this side, where any attack would most likely be expected. There are two wards enclosed with stone walls, and the inner occupies the site of the twelfth century ringwork, with a rock-cut ditch drawn across the neck of the promontory. Part, or all, of the inner ward was enclosed with a crude wall of stones laid in clay, which predate the thirteenth century defences and might conceivably have formed part of Gerald's castle.

A modern bridge crosses the deep ditch separating both wards, and at the bottom the excavated foundations of Medieval bridges of different periods can be seen. The inner ward is entered through a ruined rectangular gatehouse, which is overshadowed by two

72

great round towers that formed the principal defensive feature of Earl William's castle. Both towers have four floors reached by newel stairs contained in the thick walls, with access along passages to the gatehouse and a garderobe turret overlooking the gorge. Architectural details indicate that the east tower was built first, followed, after a short interval, by its slightly larger western companion. There is a clear break in the curtain wall between the towers and it seems likely that the builders had a change of plan; perhaps the towers were originally meant to stand closer together, so that the existing postern gate between them would have formed the principal entrance.

The remaining walls around the inner and outer wards were built in several stages during the course of the thirteenth century, and in 1377 Edward III had a large tower constructed at the very tip of the promontory. This part of the castle is now so badly ruined that the form and layout of the tower can only be guessed at; apparently it had a D-shaped front overlooking the steep drop to the river. Aside from the rather basic rooms in the various towers, domestic accomodation was supplemented by a number of stone, or timber-framed, buildings set against the inner walls. Excavations have also revealed the footings of more buildings and two simple gate-towers in the outer ward.

Refs: Brut / CADW.

DINEFWR (SN 611 217)

History. Dinefwr was the seat of the princes of west Wales, the ancestral stronghold of the ancient kingdom of Deheubarth, and main powerbase of The Lord Rhys. For these reasons alone the castle has acheived an almost mythical place in the Welsh conciousness, despite the fact that this poorly understood building has been neglected and overgrown for many years, and is only now being restored prior to public access.

According to tradition Dinefwr was founded in the Dark Ages by Rhodri Mawr or Hywel Dda, but recently doubts have been expressed about this, and it is possible that

Dinefwr: This view of the inner ward shows the stunted round keep partly enclosed by the remains of the curtain wall.

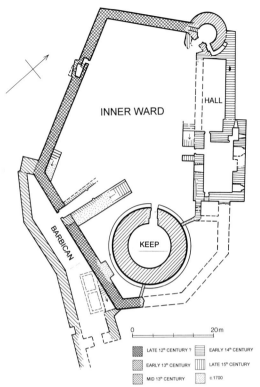

INNER WARD

HALL

BARBICAN

KEEP

0   20m

LATE 12ᵗʰ CENTURY ?   EARLY 14ᵗʰ CENTURY
EARLY 13ᵗʰ CENTURY   LATE 15ᵗʰ CENTURY
MID 13ᵗʰ CENTURY   c.1700

Plan of the inner ward of Dinefwr.

the castle's historic past was just a literary attempt to boost the prestige of Lord Rhys in the twelfth century. Certainly, there is nothing on the hilltop today to indicate any pre-Medieval earthworks, and the earliest reference to Dinefwr is in 1163, when King Henry II confirmed Rhys's tenure of the surrounding land.

Whatever its origins, Dinefwr remained a key site for the descendants of Lord Rhys, and the castle remained in Welsh hands until 1277 (though rarely under the same owner for long). At the beginning of the thirteenth century Rhys Gryg clung tenaciously to the property, despite a setback in 1213 when his nephew, Rhys Ieuanc, launched a dramatic attack with the aid of an English army. 'And on the first assault the whole castle was taken, except for the tower. And in that all the garrison gathered together and they defended strongly with missiles and stones . . . and from without archers and crossbow-men were shooting missiles, and sappers digging, and armed knights making unbearable assaults,

till they were forced before the afternoon to surrender the tower'.

In an attempt to end such conflicts, Llywelyn Fawr convened a meeting of Welsh noblemen at Aberdyfi in 1216 to apportion the Lord Rhys's territories, and Dinefwr fell to Rhys Gryg. Unfortunately Llywelyn's growing influence proved a threat to the headstrong Rhys, and four years later he was forced to dismantle the defences to prevent the castle being used against him by the prince of Gwynedd. Such an important castle was not allowed to remain in this state for long. On his death in 1233 Rhys's lands were split between his sons; Dryslwyn went to Maredudd, and Carreg Cennen and Dinefwr passed to Rhys Mechyll. The latter died in 1244 and his inheritance passed to Rhys Fychan, but the bitter rivalry between uncle and nephew was to bring about the final disintegration of Deheubarth.

With the rise to power of Llywelyn ap Gruffudd, Maredudd sided with the prince and was installed in Dinefwr in place of Rhys Fychan, who had shown royalist leanings. Henry III attempted to seize the castle in 1257 and a huge English army, led by Rhys, marched through the Tywi valley. But at the last moment, Rhys deserted his allies, and Llywelyn used guerilla tactics to massacre the invaders. Rhys was reconciled to the prince and regained his lands, leaving the furious Maredudd in control of only Dryslwyn. Both Welsh leaders died within a few weeks of each other in 1271, and their unresolved conflict passed to their heirs. When Edward I moved against Prince Llywelyn in 1276-7, Rhys ap Maredudd, Lord of Dryslwyn, sided with the royal forces and had the pleasure of witnessing his relative Rhys Wyndod evicted from Dinefwr, though he did not gain the prized fortress for himself.

Dinefwr now passed into royal control, and chamberlains were responsible for its maintenance. Rhys seized the castle during an uprising in 1287, but it was soon reclaimed and the constable of Carreg Cennen, John Giffard, was subsequently placed in charge. Around this time Edward I founded a new town nearby, although there was a small community already in existence beside the castle; today not a trace remains of either settlement.

In 1317 Dinefwr and Dryslwyn were granted to Hugh Despenser, the ambitious favourite of the weak and pliable Edward II. Despenser's grasping ways soon brought him into conflict with other English magnates, and in the ensuing civil war (1321-2), both castles were attacked and badly damaged. A later survey described the keep to be on the point of collapse, and although the constable received money to repair the roof in 1353, the work had not been carried out by the time of his death seven years later. Further damage was sustained when the castle was besieged (but apparently not captured) by the forces of Owain Glyndŵr in 1403.

Although Dryslwyn's history came to an end around this time, Dinefwr castle lingered on, and the estate was leased in 1440 to a wealthy and an ambitious local landowner, Gruffudd ap Nicholas. Gruffudd also acquired Narberth castle, and his grandson, Sir Rhys ap Thomas, gained even more lands and castles by shrewdly supporting the winning side at Bosworth in 1485. The former importance of Dinefwr now waned, and Sir Rhys built a new house for his family within the borough of Newtown. This mansion, now much restored and enlarged, is owned by the National Trust. Even though the old castle was left to moulder away, the enterprising owners of the house found a new use for the crumbling ruin, and built a summerhouse on top of the keep.

Architecture. Despite the tenacious grip of tradition, there is nothing on-site to suggest any ancient fortifications at Dinefwr, and even the outer earthworks (sometimes claimed to be Iron Age) follow the line of the curtain walls so closely that they must be contemporary. The castle occupies the highest part of a steep hill above the Tywi valley, with rock-cut ditches protecting all but the naturally strong southern flank. On the eastern approach a large and irregular

outer ward once lay, but only a few fragments of walls can now be seen, including the foundations of a square gatehouse.

The inner ward is virtually intact apart from a missing length of the east wall (lost to modern quarrying of the inner ditch), and the plan consists of a pentagonal enclosure with a circular keep, a round flanking tower, and a rectangular block of domestic apartments on the north side. The rounded layout suggests the twelfth century castle was a partial ringwork, but excavation would really be needed to find out what was here originally.

On architectural grounds the great keep can be dated to the period 1220-40, and is virtually identical to the towers built by the English at Bronllys, Skenfrith and Tretower further east. In all likelihood the tower was built by Rhys Gryg after the events of 1213 – but how old is the surrounding curtain wall? The plan is very similar to Dryslwyn (where Rhys also built a round keep), but there the walls are clearly secondary work; here there are clues which suggest that the walls were standing before the tower was built. It would be nice to be able to identify work dating to the reign of the Lord Rhys, for it seems unlikely that the great leader never carried out any re-building at his ancestral fortress. However, the pointed form of the entrance arch is typically thirteenth century, and so perhaps all of the early masonry can be attributed to Rhys Gryg. The outer ward is an addition, but must also be Welsh work of the thirteenth century, and the only other major building is the fourteenth century north range.

Access to the inner ward is along a narrow barbican fronted by a square gatetower, and recent excavations have revealed the foundations of a small building just inside the entrance. The inner entrance was altered and blocked at some point to form a smaller door, with a long passageway behind defended by arrowslits. The entrance was further modified when the stair to the summerhouse was built.

Originally there would have been stone or timber buildings lining the inner walls of the courtyard, but all have been demolished and

Dinefwr: A bird's-eye view of the inner ward in the fourteenth century. In the foreground the ditch separating the outer ward, and a gatehouse leading to the barbican can be seen. The appearance of the upper part of the round keep is conjectural and based on better preserved examples elsewhere in south Wales.

only a few windows at first floor level remain to mark their former existence. Just beside the entrance is a small square turret, and at the north-west corner of the courtyard is a more effective round tower that appears to be a thirteenth century addition. A doorway in the upper room of the tower once led to the north wall-walk, but this entire side of the castle was replaced by a large, two storeyed hall block and solar tower in the fourteenth century. This work may have been carried out by Hugh Despenser, or the chamberlains as part of the programme of repairs needed after the riot of 1322. The hall is now very badly ruined, but the solar is surprisingly intact and contains a basement, two upper chambers, and a garderobe turret. This building was extensively altered by Sir Rhys ap Thomas in the late fifteenth century.

The whole of the inner ward is dominated by the great round keep, which stands only 9m high, but 14m in diameter. This squat appearance is in contrast to the other keeps of this period, and must be due to the subsequent removal of the upper floors. An entrance has been cut through to the gloomy basement, and from inside it is possible to look up and see the outlines of a blocked window and door on the first floor. The keep was originally entered from this level along a timber bridge from the adjacent curtain wall, and perhaps a blocked stairway in the thickness of the wall led up to the residential chambers on the vanished upper floors.

At what time the keep was truncated is not known for certain. It may have been in the fourteenth century as a result of the damage caused in the Despenser riot; but perhaps a more likely period is in the early eighteenth century, when the little round summerhouse was added on top. From this lofty eyrie the residents of Newton House could gaze with admiration over the acres of Capability Brown parkland beyond the ivy-covered walls.

Refs: Brut / HKW / RCAHM (1917) / King / Griffith.

DRYSLWYN (SN 554 204)

History. Until recently all that could be seen of Dryslwyn castle was a series of earthworks on a hilltop, crowned with jagged stumps of masonry. Now, after years of excavation and consolidation work, the foundations of this great Welsh fortress have been brought to light. Despite its size, Dryslwyn is rarely mentioned in the Chronicles, and its origin is obscure. On archaeological evidence it was built in the early thirteenth century by Rhys Gryg as a powerbase to supplement his contested hold on nearby Dinefwr. The history of the two castles is closely linked, and has already been outlined in the above text on Dinefwr.

In 1287 Rhys's grandson, Rhys ap Maredudd, led a rebellion against the Crown, and a large English army was quickly assembled to enforce the peace. For several weeks Dryslwyn was battered by huge stones thrown by a siege machine, and a detachment of soldiers attempted to bring down the walls of the chapel by tunnelling under the foundations. Unfortunately the men were buried alive when the mine collapsed prematurely. Despite this dreadful setback the castle was eventually taken, though Rhys had already escaped to his last stronghold at Emlyn.

English constables were now appointed to guard the castle, and repairs costing more than £300 were carried out to strengthen the damaged building. More repairs were needed after further damage caused in the Despenser riot. In 1403 Owain made Dryslwyn his base for an attack on the neighbouring castles. Archaeological evidence suggests that Dryslwyn was deliberately demolished in the early fifteenth century, presumably by the English forces once the rebellion was over.

Architecture. The castle occupies the uneven summit of a great rocky knoll rising above the pastures of the Tywi valley. On the northern side of the hilltop lay the Medieval town, defended by stone walls and a gate, and which reached greatest prosperity in the early fourteenth century with an estimated 37 burgages. The foundations and building platforms of many houses can be clearly seen.

On the very summit of the hill stand the remains of the oldest stonework here, a round keep, which probably had two upper floors and a basement, and would have resembled the better-preserved example at Dinefwr. Next to be built was a stone wall around the inner ward, which enclosed an irregular area of sloping land. Within the courtyard stood a

Dryslwyn castle: this aerial view shows the inner ward under excavation, with the powerful earthworks of the town defences in the foreground. The foundations of several houses can just be made out.

(Crown Copyright: RCAHMW)

simple hall block containing a basement store, and a large residential chamber on the upper floor warmed by an open hearth. This phase of building work can be ascribed to Rhys Gryg (d.1233). Around the middle of the thirteenth century Maredudd ap Rhys built an outer ward to defend the entrance approach, and added another hall block to the inner ward. His son, Rhys, probably completed the outer defence works by adding yet another ward with a square gatehouse at its furthest point. The outer wards have yet to be fully excavated, but the foundations of several buildings and two gates can be seen in the long grass.

Rhys also modified the simple entrance gate to the inner ward, added a small chapel tower on the side facing the river, and greatly extended the domestic accommodation within the inner ward. When complete, Dryslwyn was the largest native castle in south Wales, and a rival to the more ambitious building schemes of the princes of Gwynedd.

Refs: Brut / HKW / Griffith / Avent.

HAVERFORDWEST (SM 953 157)

History. Haverfordwest town has long outgrown the boundaries of the little settlement established here in the protective shadow of a twelfth century castle. According to tradition the founder was the Earl of Pembroke, Gilbert de Clare, but in all likelihood the original builder was Tancard, one of the Flemish settlers introduced into this region by Henry I around 1108. Tancard's castle lay on the end of a rocky ridge overlooking an established crossing point of the Cleddau (the ford of the place-name), and although not a trace of this early fort remains, the rounded layout of the inner ward suggests it was a ringwork.

78

When Gerald of Wales visited Haverfordwest in 1188, Tancard's son, Richard, was castellan, and Gerald recounted a tale in which a prisoner in one of the towers managed to gain his freedom after taking three children hostage. One of the children was probably Richard's son, who later fell foul of King John and was dispossessed. There is no record of any successful Welsh attack, although Llywelyn Fawr attempted a siege in 1217 and was bought off. Three years later he returned and burnt the town. The castle passed to the Marshals, then to William de Valence, and finally to Humphrey de Bohun, Earl of Hereford. In 1263 Earl Humphrey granted the townsfolk the right to levy tolls to pay for the building of a wall around the settlement, but although the line of the defences is known, not a trace remains above ground today.

Queen Eleanor acquired the castle in 1289 and from then on it was held by friends of the royal family and high ranking peers. Owain Glyndŵr failed to take Haverfordwest, but luck ran out in the Civil War when the castle changed hands twice, and was afterwards demolished by the townsfolk on Cromwell's orders. The locals were too impoverished by war and disease to do much damage, but unfortunately the surviving remains suffered further depredations when a prison was built inside in 1779. A later prison building now houses the County Records Office and museum.

Architecture. Excavation and consolidation work in recent years has preserved the remaining Medieval features of the castle, but alas, the various demolishings and rebuildings carried out between the seventeenth and nineteenth centuries have reduced the castle to a gutted shell. A study of the surviving remains, coupled with a valuable survey compiled in 1577 can enable us to envisage the appearance of Haverfordwest castle prior to destruction in the Civil War.

Haverfordwest castle.

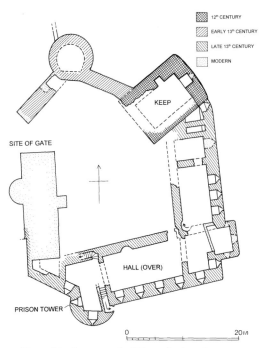

12ᵗʰ CENTURY
EARLY 13ᵗʰ CENTURY
LATE 13ᵗʰ CENTURY
MODERN

KEEP

SITE OF GATE

HALL (OVER)

PRISON TOWER

0   20ₘ

Plan of the inner ward of Haverfordwest.

A large oval outer ward lay on the western side of the ridge, and was enclosed by a stone wall studded with four small towers and a gatehouse. This gate had two portcullises, and contained a basement prison cell and a first floor room used as an exchequer. Only a stable was listed in the 1577 survey, but there must have been other buildings in the courtyard originally.

The entrance to the inner ward has vanished and its place taken by an eighteenth century Governor's House. The survey mentions two lodges on either side of the gate, suggesting this was a typical twin-towered gatehouse like the ones at Llansteffan and Kidwelly, but it also contained a postern under the entrance passage, 'made for some privy waye into the towne'. The survey then mentions a round tower on one side of the gate, but it is not certain if part of the gatehouse is meant, or

Haverfordwest: This reconstruction shows the inner ward as it might have appeared after re-building by Queen Eleanor in the late thirteenth century. The rectangular keep which is all that remains of the twelfth century fortress can be seen at the back. The form of the gatehouse is conjectural, and documentary evidence alone suggests the possible existence of the adjacent round tower.

80

(as shown in the reconstruction drawing) there was a flanking tower at the south-west corner. Two other round towers survive, that on the north side now inaccessible and much altered for use as part of the prison. The south tower contains three small chambers above a dark basement cell, and was described in 1577 as a *'strong prison house'*.

Against the inner walls stood a range of two storeyed buildings with the principal rooms (hall, chapel, kitchen, private chambers) on the first floor and graced with a series of spacious windows. At the most secure edge of the site, overlooking the steep drop to the ford, is a fragment of a rectangular keep embedded in the later masonry. Perhaps this three storeyed tower was here when Gerald visited Haverfordwest in 1188? It is the oldest remaining stonework, and appears to retain a vaulted basement now inaccessible and buried in rubble. The crude-looking north tower and adjoining stretch of curtain wall could belong to the early part of the thirteenth century, but most of the Medieval fabric was built in a fairly short period at the end of the century.

For some unclear reason, Queen Eleanor took a fancy to distant Haverfordwest, and acquired the castle through a land exchange with Humphrey de Bohun in 1289. Building work to transform the fortress into a royal residence must have started immediately, for the queen died the following year and her executors had to repay a loan of £400 for the *'operations at Haverford'*. This reconstruction must have gone on long after that date, and while it is unlikely that Eleanor ever resided here, a little weed-grown courtyard beside the towering walls was still remembered in 1577 as *'the Queen's Arbour'*.

Refs: Brut / Gerald / HKW / AC 1903 & 1922 / Soulsby.

KIDWELLY (SN 409 070)

History. The stately shell of Kidwelly castle is a far cry from the simple earth and timber fort built on this site almost 900 years ago by Roger, Bishop of Salisbury, to command the surrounding district. In 1106 the king's ally, Hywel ap Gronw, was murdered and Henry I granted the Welshman's lands to his able and ambitious minister. Roger's ringwork lay on a ridge above the tidal reaches of the Gwendraeth river, so that supplies could be brought in by boat if the overland routes were in enemy control.

In 1136 Gwenllian, wife of Gruffudd ap Rhys, valiantly led a Welsh force against the castle, but the Normans were victorious and Gwenllian was killed in battle. The name of Maurice de Londres, lord of Ogmore in Glamorgan, is mentioned in documents of the time, and when Bishop Roger died in 1139 Maurice appears to have gained control of the castle. Kidwelly remained with the de Londres family until the male line died out in the early thirteenth century, but their tenure was not undisputed. Lord Rhys was in control by 1190, and in 1215 the castle was destroyed by his son, Rhys Gryg. The de Londres heiress, Hawise, married first Walter de Breos and then Patrick de Chaworth in 1244, and it was only after this second marriage that the Welsh grip on Kidwelly was finally shaken off.

In 1257 the Welsh destroyed the town but failed to take the castle, and the forces of Owain Glyndŵr met with similar failure in 1403 (although the gatehouse was badly damaged). By then Kidwelly was Crown property, for in 1291 the de Chaworth heiress had married Edmund, Earl of Lancaster, and all the Lancastrian possessions became royal holdings on the accession of Earl Henry Bolingbroke as Henry IV in 1399. Henry VII granted Kidwelly to his loyal supporter Sir Rhys ap Thomas, but it was back with the Crown in 1531 when his grandson was executed for treason. The castle later passed to the Earls of Cawdor (who also owned Carreg Cennen), but by then the once mighty fortress was a mouldering ruin.

Kidwelly: The imposing gatehouse to the castle.

Kidwelly: the remains of the town gate.

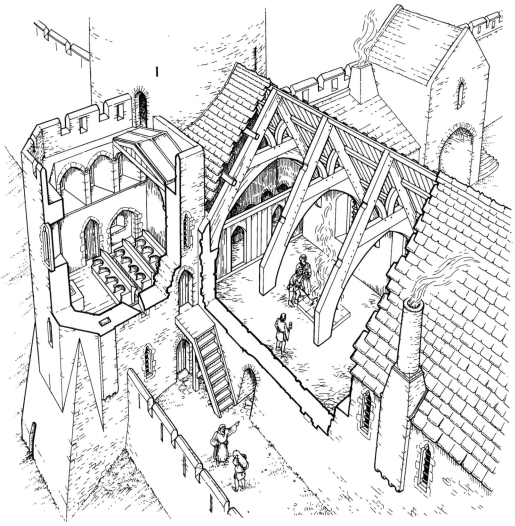

Kidwelly: A cutaway reconstruction of the great hall within the inner ward. The steeply pitched roof was supported on massive timbers, and the hall was heated by an open hearth on the floor. The chimney on the right served the private rooms. On the left the fourteenth century chapel tower can be seen, and just behind the hall the kitchen and inner gate can be glimpsed.

Architecture. Kidwelly is one of the largest and strongest castles in south Wales, and recent investigations have shown that the structure is more complex than previously thought. The castle started off as a large partial ringwork backing onto the steep slope above the river. A stone wall was later built along the crest of the curving rampart, but when, and by whom, is not known. Bishop Roger has been suggested as a likely candidate, but while he was responsible for extensive building works at his English estates, it seems unlikely that the prelate would have lavished money on a small lordship in a remote and volatile part of Wales. The wall might conceivably have been built by Lord Rhys in the 1190s, or by the English when they were back in possession early the following century.

Between 1270 and 1280 the brothers Payn and Patrick de Chaworth built a free-standing square enclosure with round corner towers in the courtyard. Each tower has three levels of rather spartan accommodation linked by newel stairs. This inner ward was entered through a weakly defended archway (wholly inadequate for the period), which suggests that there was already a strong gatehouse on the line of the outer bank. A few years later a new curtain wall with flanking towers and a little gatehouse at the northern end, was built along the rim of the earlier bank, incorporating some of the older masonry. Three of the inner ward towers were then heightened by an extra storey to enable archers stationed on the roof to oversee the outer walls.

Early in the fourteenth century Henry of Lancaster began building a large new gatehouse at the southern end of the outer ward, to guard the principal entrance into the castle. This is a remarkable structure, by far the largest and most complex of any gatehouse in west Wales, and comparable to those found in the great Edwardian castles of Gwynedd.

Any attacker attempting to enter the outer ward would have had to cross the drawbridge, break through two sets of doors and portcullises, and avoid missiles dropped through holes in the vaulted roof. Guard-rooms with dark basement dungeons lie on either side of the passageway, and the upper two floors contain numerous small rooms and larger residential chambers. The lavish use of fireplaces and spacious windows indicate that the main chambers were among the most important in the castle, and must have been reserved for the constable and his family.

Around the same time, the residential accommodation in the inner ward was also improved by the construction of a new hall block and a splendid hexagonal chapel tower jutting out towards the river. There were further additions towards the end of the Middle Ages, when Sir Rhys ap Thomas built a second hall in the outer ward, to accommodate the increasingly sophisticated needs of the Tudor gentry.

Beyond the gates lay the Medieval borough which was probably founded by Bishop Roger around the same time as the castle. Earthworks on the north and west sides may also belong to the initial settlement, but eventually only a small area was protected by stone walls. The town rapidly grew and spread to the opposite bank of the river in the vicinity of Bishop Roger's priory church, but following the Glyndŵr rebellion the 'old' town declined. This decay no doubt spared the old town from extensive modern redevelopment, though unfortunately most of the walls have been removed. Only the south gatehouse remains, and the surprising number of doors, windows and fireplaces in this three storeyed building indicates that there were no less than nine habitable chambers – the Medieval equivalent of a block of flats!

Refs: Brut / CADW / Soulsby / Avent 1991.

LAUGHARNE (SN 303 107)

History. For many years this coastal ruin remained one of the most overgrown, inaccessible, and poorly understood castles in west Wales; extensive consolidation work and excavation has changed all this, and Laugharne has recently been re-opened to the public. The castle of Robert Courtemain at Aber Cofwy mentioned in 1116 may have been Laugharne (or else the ringwork at Llanfihangel Abercywyn), but the first certain reference occurs in 1171-72. In that year Henry II met with Lord Rhys at Laugharne and agreed a parley; but the truce only lasted until the king's death, and in 1189 the castle was among the first casualties of a Welsh uprising.

The gutted fortress was re-built, but fell again to Llywelyn Fawr in 1215. By the time Laugharne suffered its next successful Welsh attack in 1257, the territory had been acquired by the de Brian family of Devon, and, for the next century and a half, the lords of Laugharne (all confusingly called Guy) set about improving their new home. The last male heir died in 1390, and for the next century ownership of the estate was disputed among various heirs and descendants.

Laugharne: This view of the inner ward shows the site of the hall and kitchen (foreground and left), with a round tower (centre) and part of Sir John Perrot's buildings (right).

Laugharne eventually passed to the Earl of Northumberland, and in 1535 the Earl sold the lordship to Henry VIII.

Queen Elizabeth rented it out to Sir John Perrot in 1575, and nine years later confirmed his tenancy by deed of settlement. Perrot set about transforming the Medieval fortress into an elegant mansion, with a formal garden in the outer ward and a stately fountain in the courtyard. Following Perrot's attainder and ignominious death in the Tower, the castle changed hands frequently, suffering from the indifference and neglect of successive owners. After a deliberate act of vandalism in 1613, the Court of the Exchequer estimated a repair cost of more than £2000. Little was done to repair the building, and within thirty years Laugharne was to suffer the final act of vandalism by Roundhead cannonfire in the Civil War. In October 1644 the Royalist garrison endured a week-long siege before surrendering the shattered fortress to the aptly-named Major-General Rowland Laugharne.

Architecture. Nothing survives above ground of the earliest castle here, but excavations have revealed some of the ringwork ditches, and the foundations of a stone hall block in the courtyard. This building dates to the twelfth century and probably resembled the better-preserved hall at Manorbier. Around the middle of the thirteenth century Guy de Brian IV (d.c1268) swept away the older structures and re-built the inner ward along similar lines to Cilgerran – two round towers at the most vulnerable part of an oval enclosure backing against the river. The larger and better-preserved west tower seems to have been the more important of the two, and had four floors under a pointed stone dome. The entrance to the courtyard was a simple gap through the curtain wall, but Guy de Brian V (d.1307) improved this by building a projecting gatehouse of rectangular plan, with round corner turrets. Guy also built the outer ward defences including the ruined gatehouse facing the town. Sections of the curtain wall and domestic buildings on the more secure south

Laugharne: The inner ward as it might have appeared after Sir John Perrot's reconstruction in the late sixteenth century. Few of the internal buildings survive today and their conjectural appearance is based on other Tudor mansions of the period. This view should be contrasted with the drawings on page 46 showing the early development of the castle.

side of the inner ward were also re-built at this time, and the exposed south-west corner was capped by a little round tower with a spur base.

Towards the end of the fourteenth century Guy VII (d.1390) carried out further improvements to the defences, and enlarged the hall block. He also added a square tower at the south-east corner which overlooked a postern gate leading down to the beach. From this time until the late sixteenth century no further alterations took place, and the castle fell into a state of disrepair. By the time Sir John Perrot acquired the estate, the need for castles had long passed, and so he converted the old fortress into a palatial residence. The domestic accommodation was greatly improved; the Medieval hall received new windows and attic rooms, the stern gatehouse was transformed into an elegant porch, and most of the curtain walls were raised and given dummy battlements. Between the two round towers Perrot built another hall block, with a tall stair turret giving access to three floors of accommodation.

Sadly, much of Sir John's work has vanished, and a survey drawn up at the time of his downfall records some of the lost splendour. Within the little courtyard stood '*a very proper fountaine, with a stately round stairs . . . and a porch over a part thereof leading into a faire hall*'. Probably the major rooms had panelled walls hung with tapestries and arras, but now only bare masonry commemorates the former glory of Laugharne castle.

Ref: Brut / Avent / CADW.

LLANDOVERY (SN 767 343)

History. Llandovery was a Norman found-ation established by Richard fitz Pons before 1116, deep in the Welsh territory of Cantref Bychan. In that year it was attacked by Gruffudd ap Rhys, but the Welsh army failed to dislodge the invaders and only succeeded in burning the 'outer castle' or bailey. In 1158 the current owner, Walter Clifford, rashly encroached on the Lord Rhys's territory and provoked a retaliatory attack in which the castle was taken. Llandovery was briefly regained, and Henry II spent a large sum of money repairing it, but its remote location ensured the castle remained in native control during the ascendancy of the houses of Deheubarth and Gwynedd.

Even though it was not until 1276 that the English reclaimed the castle, Llandovery frequently changed hands between the warring factions. A choice episode from this sorry chronicle of internal strife happened in 1227, when Rhys Gryg was captured by his own son, and only released in exchange for the castle!

During the late twelfth century a town grew up beside the castle (there was even a short-lived Benedictine priory), but economic growth was only really possible in the more stable conditions imposed by the English Crown. Edward I granted Llandovery to John Giffard, though it was temporarily lost in the uprisings of 1282 and 1287. It was last used as a fortress during the revolt of Owain Glyndŵr, and thereafter the castle was left to decay. When John Leland passed through the area in the 1530s he failed to notice the castle, and commented only on the impoverished town.

Architecture. The castle originated as a small, but strong motte and bailey carved out of a natural rocky mound beside the river Bran, with an outer moat flooded by the Bawddwr stream. The steep sided motte is almost 10m high, and this combination of strong natural and artificial defences no doubt helped save the keep during the initial Welsh attack. Henry II ordered the refortification of Llandovery in 1160-62, and the sum involved is sufficient to account for

Llandovery: the ruins of the keep on the twelfth century motte.

some masonry work, though it is not certain if the small bailey was ever walled in stone.

The surviving masonry on the motte consists of a short length of curtain wall with a rounded corner bastion (containing a well), and a large D-shaped tower boldly projecting down the side of the mound. This tower had a dimly lit basement, with two upper residential apartments provided with windows and garderobes. Presumably the rest of the summit was occupied by some form of shell-keep, like the better-preserved example at Carmarthen.

The building of the stone defences is usually attributed to John Giffard around 1283, yet the tower is much more old-fashioned than his slightly later work at Carreg Cennen: and the fact that it was precariously built half-way down the slope strongly suggests that there was a pre-existing keep on the summit that the builders did not want to interfere with. Presumably this was King Henry's work of c1162, and it is possible that the surviving curtain wall is part of that building.

Refs: Brut / HKW / Soulsby / King / CA 1990.

LLANSTEFFAN (SN 351 101)

History. Llansteffan, along with Laugharne and Kidwelly, guarded one of the three rivers flowing into Carmarthen Bay, emphasising the importance of water-borne communication routes for the Norman invaders. The castle was probably built after Carmarthen had been re-founded further upstream in 1105, but the first mention of Llansteffan is in 1146 when it was captured by Cadell, Maredudd and Rhys ap Gruffudd, the young heirs of the house of Deheubarth.

The *Brut y Tywysogion* records how Maredudd held the castle against a Norman counter-attack: '*for a boy though he was in age, he showed none the less the action of a man . . . when the enemy saw how few were the defenders, they raised ladders against the walls, and he bore with his enemies until they were on the ladders, and then he came with his men and overturned the ladders, so that his enemies were in the ditch, many of them being slain and others put to flight*'. The English were back in possession by 1160 and

The gatehouse, Llansteffan.

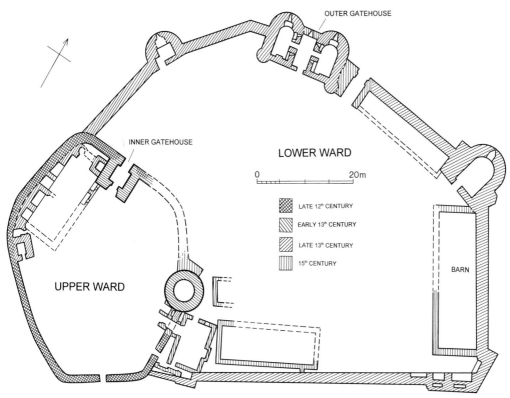

OUTER GATEHOUSE

INNER GATEHOUSE

LOWER WARD

0   20m

▨ LATE 12th CENTURY

◫ EARLY 13th CENTURY

▨ LATE 13th CENTURY

▥ 15th CENTURY

BARN

UPPER WARD

Plan of Llansteffan.

towards the close of the twelfth century Llansteffan was held by Geoffrey Marmion, whose heiress conveyed the estate to her Devonshire husband, William de Camville. The de Camvilles held Llansteffan until 1338 and most of the surviving stonework was built by them.

Llansteffan was one of the first castles destroyed by the Lord Rhys on renewing hostilities with the Crown in 1189, but the Welsh could not hold on to the district for long, and by 1192 William de Camville was back in possession and borrowing money to repair the defences. Llywelyn Fawr burnt the castle in 1215 and his grandson repeated the act in 1257, but the de Camvilles soon regained their lands and set about replacing the timber defences with stone walls and towers. In the fourteenth century Llansteffan passed to the Penres family of Gower, but when Robert de Penres was convicted of the murder of a local woman in 1370, the castle

and lands passed to the Crown. During the Glyndŵr uprising the castle was held for a time by the rebels, and subsequently passed to a succession of absentee owners. The Earl of Pembroke, Jasper Tudor, held it from 1483 to 1495 and may have been responsible for carrying out some minor alterations to the building, before it was left to crumble into decay. By the nineteenth century the overgrown walls protected nothing more pretentious than a farmyard.

Architecture. Llansteffan castle occupies a splendid coastal site on a hill south of the village, overlooking the broad expanse of the Tywi estuary. There are two wards, and the uppermost and smallest occupies the site of the Norman ringwork which was built within an Iron Age hillfort. The deep ditches and outer banks curving around the north and west sides of the castle were dug a thousand years before the Normans arrived.

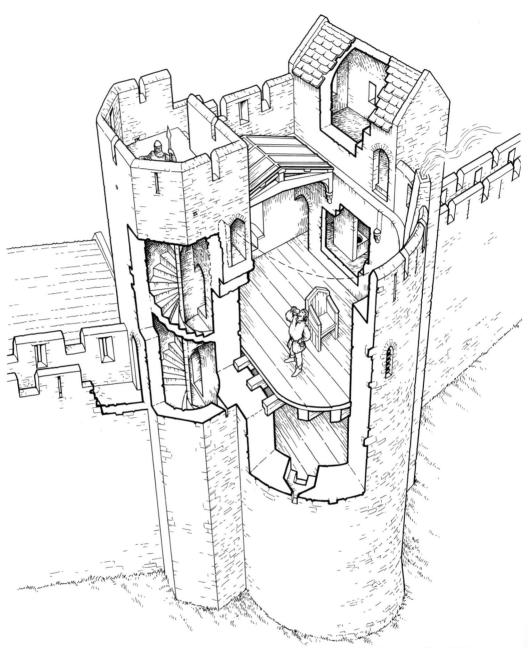

Llansteffan: The south-east tower was probably used as private rooms adjoining the hall, and this cutaway view shows the principal room on the top floor. One of the side turrets contained a stair, the other garderobes, with a little guardroom at roof level.

The present entrance is through a modest gateway (a Tudor addition) which stands in the shadow of a much more formidable gatehouse built by Geoffrey de Camville II in the 1280s. This has two guardrooms on either side of an entrance passage defended by two porcullises and murder holes in the vaulted roof. The large outer gate was blocked up when the Tudor entrance was built alongside, but above the arch a chute can be seen, through which the defenders could have poured water to prevent the wooden doors from being burnt. On the first floor there is a single large room with spacious windows overlooking the courtyard, and a garderobe in a passage off the stairs. The upper level has the same arrangements, and the decorative sculptures on the fireplaces and roof corbels add a touch of refinement not usually encountered in these grim fortresses.

Just east of the gatehouse is a well-preserved D-shaped tower with flanking turrets containing stairs and garderobes. There are fireplaces in the two upper chambers, and it is likely that this tower was used by the de Camville family as a solar. The adjacent barn is another Tudor addition, but apparently occupies the site of the hall. Excavations in the 1970s revealed the foundations of other buildings in the courtyard, some built over the ringwork ditch indicating that it no longer had any defensive purpose.

In contrast to the large outer gate, the upper ward is entered through a more modest square tower, with only a portcullis and wooden door to hold back potential attackers. Against the west wall the remains of domestic buildings and vaults inserted to support a wall-walk can be seen. The foundations of a small round keep probably date to the early thirteenth century, but the thin and flimsy curtain wall is much earlier, and was probably built by William de Camville I in 1192 to repair the devastation caused by the Lord Rhys.
Refs: Brut / CADW.

LLAWHADEN (SN 073 174)

History. Churchmen relied on more than just divine protection to safeguard their vast estates, and at Newmoat, Parc-y-castell, and Llawhaden, we can see fortifications built by men of God, rather than avaricious Norman warlords. Llawhaden was an ancient manor belonging to St Davids cathedral and it was probably Bernard (1115-48), the first Norman bishop, who built a castle here to protect the surrounding lands. Gerald of Wales visited his uncle Bishop David fitz Gerald here in 1175, but in 1192 the castle was seized by Lord Rhys. Rhys relegated control to his son, Hywel, but the Welsh had over-reached themselves, and Hywel decided to burn the castle to the ground, and retreat to more securely held territories.

Llawhaden was soon re-occupied and repaired, and there is no further record of a Welsh attack (although Llywelyn Fawr ravaged the neighbouring castles at Narberth and Wiston in 1220). During the more settled years at the close of the thirteenth century Bishop Thomas Bek (1280-93) began to re-build the castle, and established a market town beyond the gates. Bek also founded a hospice for the aged and infirm, and the ruined chapel belonging to that establishment can still be seen. There is no record of a siege during the Glyndŵr rebellion, although Henry IV ordered the castle to be put in a state of defence, and probably the last time Llawhaden witnessed any military action was in 1503, when Thomas Wyrriot of Orielton broke into the building to free a local woman imprisoned there.

Bishop Houghton's gatehouse at Llawhaden.

Llawhaden: A bird's-eye reconstruction of the Bishop's castle as it might have appeared after re-building in the late fourteenth century. The large hall block stands at the rear of the courtyard, and the two round towers at the top left were later demolished and replaced by a range of buildings.

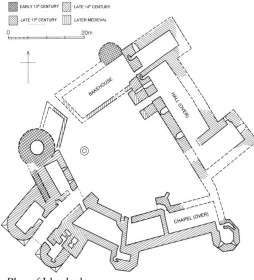

EARLY 13ᵗʰ CENTURY   LATE 14ᵗʰ CENTURY
LATE 13ᵗʰ CENTURY   LATER MEDIEVAL

0   20m

BAKEHOUSE

HALL (OVER)

CHAPEL (OVER)

Plan of Llawhaden.

Bishop Vaughan (1509-22) is believed to have carried out various repairs, but within a short time the Reformation brought sweeping changes to religious and social life in Britain, and Bishop Barlow (1536-48) moved the principal residence to Abergwili near Carmarthen. The castle was stripped of saleable materials (allegedly to support one of Barlow's illegitimate children), and in 1616 Bishop Milbourne was granted a licence to demolish what remained. In subsequent years the hilltop ruin attracted not only artists and antiquarians, but local builders as well, so that Richard Fenton complained that the *'venerable building has been plundered most shamefully and unnecessarily to supply materials for repairing the roads'*.

Architecture. Despite extensive reconstruction in later years, the great ditch of the twelfth century ringwork is still clearly visible today, as are the foundations of the first masonry defences – a circular turret and round tower linked by curtain walls – probably built in the early thirteenth century. Bishop Bek upgraded the residential accommodation in the latter part of the century by building a fine hall block on the far side of the courtyard, opposite the gate. Two projecting wings at either end of the hall contained a kitchen and private chamber on the upper floors, with vaulted storerooms below. A wooden stair provided access to the hall at first, but this was later replaced by a grand stairway crowned with a wooden porch or forebuilding.

Presumably the remainder of the enclosure was surrounded by the earlier walls and towers, but late in the fourteenth century Bishop Adam Houghton (1362-89) began an ambitious re-building scheme. The entire southern half of the castle was provided with a high curtain wall with multiangular towers, and the earlier gatehouse was extended and refaced. Only the elaborate facade of the gatehouse now remains, but the foundations of guardrooms can be seen on either side of the entrance passage, as well as the portcullis groove and one of the drawbridge pivot stones.

Against the inner walls stood a range of lavish apartments designed to accommodate the bishop's guests in some degree of comfort (for less welcome visitors there was a dungeon pit in one of the towers). One of the flanking towers contains a series of little bedrooms with garderobes, while the larger east tower has two fine octagonal chambers with vaulted roofs. Between the new apartments and older hall lay the bishop's private chapel, a large room distinguished by spacious windows and an elaborate porch.

Despite all this expenditure it seems likely that the grand scheme was never carried to completion, and the entire north-west side of the courtyard was defended only by the early thirteenth century defences. At a much later date the remaining towers and walls on this flank were demolished and replaced with two small buildings – clearly by then the threat of an attack was considered remote.
Refs: Brut / Fenton / CADW.

MANORBIER (SS 064 978)

History. Manorbier castle, once the stronghold of this minor lordship of the earldom of Pembroke, crowns the summit of a ridge in a pleasant valley on the coast. The castle was probably founded in the early years of the twelfth century by Odo de Barri, a member of a Norman family originally established at Barry in Glamorgan. The first historical reference to the place occurs in the writings of the famous cleric and chronicler, Gerald of Wales (Gerallt Gymro), the fourth son of William de Barri and Angharad de Carew. Gerald was born here in about 1146 and later described the castle as being '*excellently well defended by turrets and bulwarks*' – which in his day would have been of timber construction with a fine stone hall.

Manorbier had a relatively peaceful history. There is no record of a Welsh attack (though young Gerald fled to the church for safety during a siege on nearby Tenby in 1153), but in the 1320s the castle was broken into and allegedly ransacked during a family dispute. The de Barris retained possession until the second half of the fourteenth century, by which time all the Medieval parts of the building had been completed; its subsequent history is one of minor alterations, repairs and, ultimately, decay.

The estate was held by a succession of owners and in c1461 passed to the Crown, the castle then being granted out to various tenants. By the 1530s the buildings had become dilapidated, and the antiquary John Leland saw '*the ruines of Pirrhus Castel . . . many Walles yet standyng hole, do openly appere*'. A survey of 1618 described it as '*a ruynous castle quite decayed*'.

However, these reports could be exaggerating the condition since some of the

93

Manorbier: This reconstruction shows part of the inner ward towards the end of the thirteenth century. The Norman hall (centre) has been incorporated into a range of buildings, including a large chapel (left). The low building on the right was probably a kitchen.

buildings were adapted for use during the sixteenth century, and a large barn (subsequently converted into a house) was built in the courtyard at some point in the seventeenth century. At the time of the Civil War Manorbier was held by the Philipps family of Picton, and was re-fortified for use as a Royalist stronghold. In September 1645 the Parliamentary commander reported the capture of Carew, Manorbier and Picton castles, and the defences were slighted (fortunately on a modest scale). The picturesque ruin gained a new lease of life in the late nineteenth century when J. R. Cobb, a castle enthusiast responsible for repairing Pembroke, leased Manorbier and built a house within the courtyard.

Architecture. For such a small lordship and relatively minor ruling family, Manorbier is an exceptionally ambitious castle, a fact more apparent in earlier years when the outer ward (now reduced to insignificant fragments) would have doubled the area enclosed by the defences. Close examination of the stonework however, reveals that the castle was built piecemeal over a long period of time, and stengthened whenever the de Barris had enough cash to do so.

Hardly a trace remains of the original castle, but there is no motte here, and so the rock-cut ditch in front of the inner ward is probably all that remains of a partial ringwork. In Gerald's day the most dominating feature was the Norman hall at the furthest point of the ridge, which had probably been built by his father William in the 1140s. The rest of the courtyard was perhaps enclosed by timber palisades linked to a small and crude stone tower beside the gate. The two storeyed hall is very likely the oldest stone building remaining at any castle site in west Wales, and its plain and gloomy character reflects its original function as a residential keep. At ground level there are dark storerooms with inserted vaults, and an external stair leading up to the first floor hall. This large and lofty room was heated by a generous fireplace in the side wall, but the windows were little more than unglazed slits, and so the interior would have been very dark. Beyond a partition at one end lay a storeroom with a fairly comfortable solar above.

In the second quarter of the thirteenth century the old enclosure defences were replaced with masonry walls and two round flanking towers to guard the level approach to the gate. The entrance was just an archway with a portcullis, but this was later incorporated into a more effective square gatetower. At various times in the second half of the century the domestic accommodation was greatly improved, and some of the work was carried out by David de Barri (d.c1280), Lord Justiciar of Ireland. Using the proceeds from his more lucrative Irish estates, David built a grand chapel block in the courtyard, and later added a solar wing to link it with the older hall. From a corner of this new wing an elaborate garderobe tower was constructed, jutting out beyond the curtain walls. Within the courtyard a well and the remains of various buildings set against the inner walls can be seen, including a kitchen and barn. Another large barn stands in the outer ward, but only a few shattered walls and some flanking towers remain of the defences of this part of the castle. In the valley below the castle the remains of a mill and a dovecot can be seen, two valuable assets to any manorial residence.

Refs: Gerald / Leland / AC 1970.

The approach to the inner ward, Manorbier.

NARBERTH (SN 109 143)

History. According to the ancient Welsh folk tales *The Mabinogion*, Narberth was the court of Pwyll, Prince of Dyfed, but such a legendary palace would have been very different from the grim Medieval fortress built here by the Mortimers in the thirteenth century. The historical 'castle in Arberth' makes its first recorded appearance in 1116 when it was destroyed by Gruffudd ap Rhys. It is thought to have been founded by Stephen Perrot, one of the Norman warlords introduced into Pembrokeshire by Henry I, and the Perrot family were subsequently to figure largely in the affairs of west Wales.

The castle was re-built, but fell to Rhys Ieuanc and Maelgwn ap Rhys in 1215, and was again destroyed in 1220 by Llywelyn Fawr. By this time the territory had been acquired by the Marshals, and Henry III

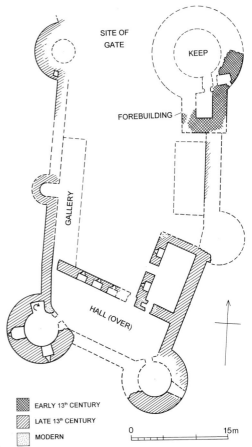

Plan of Narberth.

Only fragments remain of the keep at Narberth, but it would have resembled the more intact towers shown on page 49.

exhorted the locals to help William Marshal II rebuild the strongholds damaged in the attack. With the death of the last male heir the extensive Marshal inheritance was split up among various heiresses, and Narberth (along with St Clears) passed first to William de Breos (d.1230) and then in 1247 to the powerful Mortimer family. In 1257 the castle was again destroyed in a Welsh attack, led by Llywelyn ap Gruffudd.

Many historians claim that the original castle of Narberth was the ringwork at Templeton, some 3km to the south, and that the existing fortress was not built until after Llywelyn's attack. In fact, there is no evidence to support this tenacious belief; the existing stonework dates in part to the early thirteenth century and appears to overlie an older earthwork.

Narberth was a long way from the Mortimer powerbase in the Welsh Marches, and yet most of the surviving structure was built by them and the growth of an adjoining town was encouraged. In the fifteenth century the property passed to Richard, Duke of York, nephew of the last Mortimer heir, who was soon to become embroiled in the Wars of the Roses. Gruffudd ap Nicholas of Dinefwr acquired the castle from the duke, but it passed to Richard's son and heir Edward IV, and remained a Crown possession until Henry VIII granted the lordship to Sir Rhys ap Thomas in 1516.

However, the castle was not to remain with the Dinefwr family for long, and following the execution of his grandson for alleged treason, all of Rhys's vast estates were seized by the king. Narberth eventually ended up with the affluent Barlows of Slebech Hall, and although the building was said to be 'decayed and wasted' in 1609, there is a tradition that part was inhabited as late as 1677, before it was finally left to rot away. It is not certain if Narberth ever played a part in the Civil War, but just below the castle on the south side is a triangular earthwork that may be a defensive feature of the period.

Architecture. Very little of the building remains intact today, and only part of the south domestic range with two flanking towers survive to any great height. Excavation would be needed to unravel the plan of this little-understood fortress, but a detailed survey drawn up in 1539 can be used in conjunction with the existing ruins to provide a tentative reconstruction.

Narberth castle lies on a narrow sloping ridge below the town, and consists of a long rectangular enclosure with four round towers and a large keep. The entrance lay on the north side facing the town, but this is now the most ruined part of the site and not a scrap remains of the gatehouse. There were two low chambers on either side of the gate, with a single large room on the first floor. This arrangement is typical of the twin-towered gatehouses we see at Llansteffan and Newcastle Emlyn, but it is also possible that the gate more closely resembled the one at Pembroke; a rectangular block overlooked by adjacent towers. The survey states that the keep lay 'over the east part of the said gatehouse', and the foundations of one of the flanking towers can be seen in the undergrowth very close to where the gate stood.

The 'Great Tower' or keep has been reduced to a solitary upstanding fragment, but it is, nevertheless, an informative fragment. There are garderobe shafts, fireplaces, and window holes, and the surviving details indicate a structure very similar in age and style to the early thirteenth century keep at Dinefwr. It contained a 'great deep dungeon' and three upper chambers, with two small turrets (stairs?) rising above the battlements. One of these is shown on an engraving by the Buck brothers dated 1740. The tower was reached by a flight of 29 steps housed within a projecting square tower or forebuilding, which had a little vaulted room at dungeon level.

Just north of the keep the ridge rises to a flat-topped mound now very overgrown and cut into by modern houses on one side. This must have been included in the defensive scheme (perhaps as a barbican or small outer ward) and in fact looks very much like the remains of a motte. The Buck engraving appears to show some masonry remains on the mound top. South of the keep the foundations of a two storeyed building that once contained a parlour and chamber can be seen, and next to this stood a small, three storeyed flanking tower.

From here on the castle is better preserved, and the next block of buildings contained a vaulted pantry with a first floor 'great chamber' or solar. The hall lay across the south end of the courtyard, with a kitchen on the ground floor, and three storeyed round towers at the two outer corners. The south-east tower contained a bakehouse at ground level and a little chapel above. Regarding the hall, only the corbels to support the floor beams and a few ragged window openings can be seen, but it must have been a large and grand chamber, similar to the one at Carew. There was another range of buildings (possibly half-timbered) on the west side of the courtyard, with a gallery above leading to a small, round turret.

The surviving remains cannot be closely dated, although the absence of spurs on the main flanking towers recall the inner wards of Kidwelly and Laugharne, and might suggest a similar construction period (c1260-1280). The round keep is possibly earlier, and was apparently built on, or beside, a Norman motte. It is generally considered that the adjoining town was undefended, but the Buck engraving shows a square tower near the church. Was this the gatehouse to Elizabethan Plas House, or the entrance to the Medieval town? Could Narberth (like Laugharne) have had timber defences supplemented with stone gates? Only careful excavations at some future date may solve this riddle.

Refs: Brut / Fenton / AC 1865 / RCAHM 1925 / Soulsby / DAT.

NEVERN (SN 082 401)

History. In the early years of the twelfth century a Devonshire knight, Robert fitz Martin, landed in northern Pembrokeshire and established a Marcher lordship centred on the Welsh commote of Cemais. To defend his new territory Robert built a strong castle at Nevern, and his followers spread out in the ensuing years, building minor outposts and turning Cemais into the most heavily castled commote in west Wales.

Nevern apparently remained in Norman hands until 1191, when it was held by William fitz Martin, a son-in-law of Lord Rhys through a politic marriage with his daughter, Angharad. Rhys had extended his control as far as neighbouring Cilgerran, and found Nevern too tempting a target to miss. Ignoring family ties (and despite having sworn an oath to the contrary), Rhys seized Nevern; it is doubtful whether he appreciated the irony of the situation when his own rebellious sons imprisoned him briefly at the castle three years later. English control was

Nevern: in the foreground the outer bank and ditch can be seen, with the tree-covered motte in the background.

98

Nevern: A bird's-eye reconstruction of this complex motte and bailey castle. The exact position of the entrance is conjectural, as is the appearance of the two towers, which now lie in utter ruin.

not fully established in Cemais until 1204 when William Marshal captured Cilgerran from the Welsh, but it is not certain that Nevern was ever re-occupied. By 1215 a castle at nearby Newport had become the new fitz Martin stronghold.

The great earthworks nevertheless remained a prominent feature of the landscape for centuries. The Elizabethan historian George Owen wrote that although the castle was '*utterly defaced, yet doth the seat thereof show at what strength it was in times past, being seated on a high hill . . . and strengthened with a mighty dyke hewn out of the main rock*'.

Architecture. Nevern is one of the largest and most complex earthwork castles in west Wales and, despite various theories put forward, the development of the site will only be understood by excavation at some future date. Fitz Martin's stronghold occupies a roughly triangular area of land on the edge of a rocky gorge above the ancient Celtic church

of St Brynach. The natural defences were supplemented by a massive right-angled bank 8m high and fronted by a deep, boggy ditch. An additional rampart and ditch guard the north flank.

At the corner where all the banks meet is an irregular motte, up to 12.3m high, with the foundations of a round tower 8m in diameter on the summit. This mound has every appearance of being an addition, and was probably heaped up over an existing earthwork. In the east corner of the bailey, where the natural defences are at their most advantageous, an inner ward was formed by cutting a ditch through the shaly rock and isolating a small, level platform. This is surrounded by a low stone wall and encloses a ruined tower about 10m square.

All these features are unlikely to be contemporary and, as previously mentioned, without archaeological dating evidence the development of the castle can only be conjectured. The right-angled banks may have been part of an Iron Age hillfort, with the motte being a Norman addition. Some, or all of the masonry defences could well be the work of Lord Rhys after 1191, though the round tower on the motte is more typical of the early thirteenth century, and might suggest a short-lived re-occupation of Nevern by the fitz Martins.

Refs: Brut / Owen / AC 1951 / JPHS 1989.

NEWCASTLE EMLYN (SN 311 407)

History. Around 1240 Henry III divided the territory of Emlyn in the Teifi valley between Walter Marshal, and Maredudd ap Rhys Gryg. The western portion controlled from Cilgerran went to Marshal, while the eastern half was granted to Maredudd, who built the New Castle to defend his lands. At the time of his son's rebellion Emlyn was in English hands, but with the fall of Dryslwyn, Rhys ap Maredudd led a surprise attack and seized the castle in November 1287.

By the end of the year a large English army was making a slow and arduous trek along the valley from Cardigan, bringing along the great stone-throwing machine that

Newcastle Emlyn gatehouse.

had caused so much damage at Dryslwyn. This engine (probably a trebuchet or mangonel) was dragged by a team of sixty oxen, and finally reached the castle on January 10th. After a six-day siege the castle was over-run and many of the defenders killed, but Rhys had already slipped away and remained at large until April. His execution brought Welsh rule to an end in Deheubarth.

Between 1288 and 1382 the castle was in royal hands and a long drawn-out series of repairs and re-building work is recorded in official documents. A small town grew up outside the gates, rivaling the older borough of Adpar across the river, but the damage caused in the Glyndŵr uprising brought a halt to the urban development. Sir Rhys ap Thomas acquired the dilapidated castle at the end of the fifteenth century and restored the building for use as a hunting lodge, but with the execution of his grandson, the estate passed to the Crown. The New Castle last saw military action in the Civil War when it was garrisoned for the king, and suffered a two week siege by Parliamentarian forces in 1644. The meagre remains suggest that the Roundheads were particularly thorough in slighting the defences.

Architecture. The castle was built on a ridge within a loop of the river Teifi, and so all the man-made defences were massed on the only flank open to attack. Maredudd's work probably consisted of the earthwork outer ward, with a smaller inner ward of triangular plan enclosed by a stone wall. However, almost all of the masonry visible today is likely to date from the early fourteenth century, with the exception of the prominent bastion in front of the gate, which is probably a relic of the Civil War period.

Building accounts of the fourteenth century record some of the works carried out by the Crown after the revolt of Rhys ap Maredudd. There was a wooden barbican beyond the outer gate '*built of great timbers and boards*', and also timber brattices or hourdings on three corners of the inner ward.

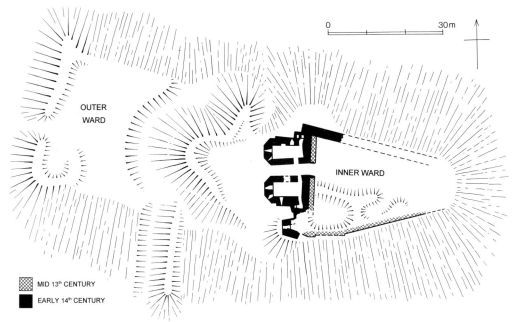

OUTER WARD

INNER WARD

MID 13ᵗʰ CENTURY

EARLY 14ᵗʰ CENTURY

Plan of Newcastle Emlyn.

Today the principal feature of the castle is the inner gatehouse, robbed of its defensive capabilities by Sir Rhys ap Thomas. There is no sign of a ditch, drawbridge, or portcullis, and the arrowslits have been opened out to form spacious windows. The north chamber was described in a survey of 1532 as a *'Porter's lodge with prisonhowse under'*, and this dark vaulted dungeon was found in recent excavations. The upper floor is now badly ruined and the internal arrangement cannot be recovered, but according to the survey there were five rooms with a stair leading up to the battlements.

The Wardrobe Tower is a small multi-angular turret on the south corner of the inner ward and is just as ruined as the gatehouse. It contained two or three little rooms, and may have been an addition to the earlier curtain wall. A few foundations and grassy mounds outlining the site of the principal domestic buildings are the only remains of the rest of the castle.

Work on the gatehouse was in progress c1320 and appears to have been completed c1348. At the same time a new hall and two buildings were constructed in the courtyard. From the survey carried out in 1532 it is clear that all the buildings stood against the south curtain wall and (moving eastwards from the gatehouse) consisted of a cellar with a large hall above; then a stairway with a chapel over; next came a vaulted larder with a kitchen on the first floor. There was also a garderobe block here, which rose above the battlements to form *'a little tower to view and see the country'*. At the furthest end of the inner ward stood a 'privy kitchen' with two first floor rooms, and a 'wardrobe chamber' (garderobe?) over.

Outside the castle walls (but still within the protective loop of the river) stood ancillary buildings including a bakehouse, brewery and hay-shed, and within a mile of the town lay a well-stocked deer park where Sir Rhys and his retinue could indulge in the Tudor pastime of decimating the local wildlife.

Refs: RCAHM 1917 / HKW / Soulsby / CA 1987, 1992 / Griffith.

NEWPORT (SN 057 388)

History. The 'new port' and castle of Cemais was founded by William fitz Martin after Nevern had been captured by the Welsh. The old hilltop motte and bailey was abandoned in favour of a new site at the estuary of the river Nyfer, which provided a more reliable maritime communication and supply route. William not only built a new castle here (a large ringwork rather than a motte), but also founded a church and borough, which reached greatest prosperity by the fifteenth century.

When this move took place is not known, but it must have been before 1215 when the castle of Trefdraeth (Newport) was burnt by Llywelyn Fawr. There is also uncertainty about the significance of a small ringwork at the lower end of the town – was this William's first castle before he moved to a loftier site beside the church? Or is it a relic of an earlier Norman settlement? Whichever site was in occupation, it was destroyed again by the Welsh in 1257, and it was only after this attack that masonry was added to the ringwork beside the church.

The re-built gatehouse at Newport.

With the death of the last Fitzmartin heir in 1325 the estate passed to the Audley family, with whom it remained until acquired by William Owen of Henllys in 1543. William's son, the famous historian George Owen (1552-1613), described Newport as '*a strong and large castle, moated, garreted, and with towers, and having a large court within*'. But by then it was in ruins, and may have been uninhabited ever since the Glyndŵr revolt. The castle continued to decay until the mid nineteenth century when a private house was built within the remains of the gatehouse, and some repairs carried out. The site is still in private ownership, and some further repairs have been done. The RCAHM recently published a detailed survey of the remains.

Architecture. The builders of Newport castle took advantage of a steep ridge between two streams to construct a large ringwork 55m across, and surrounded by a deep ditch and counterscarp bank. In later years the ditch was flooded for use as a millpond. The stonework was probably added sometime towards the end of the thirteenth century, but only excavation will confirm this. The summit of the ringwork bank was surrounded by a curtain wall with three flanking towers and a twin-towered gatehouse, all built projecting down the slopes of the mound. Only a single wall remains of the north-west or Hunter's Tower, and the Kitchen Tower on the south-west side has vanished apart from a Victorian dungeon constructed in the rubble.

More survives of the third and principal tower guarding the south-east side. This D-shaped tower with spurs stands to first floor level, and although provided with plenty of windows and garderobes, there are no fireplaces. Presumably the expected residential chamber was on the missing upper floor. Adjoining the tower is a square building with a surprisingly fine undercroft, the rib vaulting supported on a central octagonal pillar. Perhaps this room was the crypt of a first floor chapel? Only one of the gatehouse towers remains standing, and this has a rounded front rising from a spur base to

THE SOUTH VIEW OF NEWPORT-CASTLE, IN THE COUNTY OF PEMBROKE.

THIS Castle was call'd by the Britains Trevdraeth, it is in the Hundred of Kemaes, and is situated on the River Nevern. It is said to have been built by the Posterity of Martin of Tours, and was their chief Seat. A.D. 1215, it was demolish'd by Llewellyn Prince of South Wales, being then possess'd by the Flemings: In process of time it came to the Family of the Owens, who also became Lords of Kemaes; and for want of Issue Male it fell to John Laugharne of Laurithan Gent. and to M.r Lloyd of Bronwith, who are the present Proprietors.

Sam.l & Nath.l Buck del et sculp. Publish'd according to Act of Parliament April 5 1740.

Newport castle as seen by the Buck brothers in 1740.

an octagonal parapet (an unusual feature also seen at Benton). The remaining Medieval masonry was incorporated into a Gothic-style house, built c1860 and further extended at the end of the ninteenth century.

Refs: Brut / Owen / RCAHM 1925, 1992 / Soulsby.

PEMBROKE (SM 982 016)

History. From its origin as an eleventh century ringwork, Pembroke castle developed into one of the strongest and most powerful fortresses in the whole of Wales. Even today, after centuries of warfare and depredation of the elements, Pembroke is still an impressive architectural and military achievement.

Led by Roger de Montgomery, the Normans marched to this site across Wales in 1093 and built the first castle here on a rocky promontory above the river – a triangular area of the headland fortified with a bank, ditch and timber palisade. Roger's son, Arnulf, arrived by sea and was given custody of the new fort. Pembroke and Rhydygors were the only west Wales castles to survive a Welsh uprising the following year, but, according to the *Brut y Tywysogion*,

Pembroke was looted in 1096 by the Welsh, who ravaged the surrounding lands and *'returned home with vast spoil'*. In fact, the attack was probably foiled by a cunning ploy instigated by Gerald de Windsor. Arnulf was deprived of his possessions in 1102 for taking part in a rebellion against Henry I, and Pembroke was granted to Gerald.

King Stephen subsequently gave the castle to Gilbert de Clare (d.1148) and his son, Richard 'Strongbow' (d.1176) made Pembroke an important embarkation point for his conquests in Ireland. The great William Marshal acquired all the de Clare estates on his marriage to Richard's heiress in 1189, and the transformation of the ringwork into a substantial stone fortress began. The rather luckless Marshal dynasty came to an abrupt end in 1245, and with no male heir the vast inheritance was fragmented among the relatives of the female heirs.

Pembroke eventually passed to William de Valence (d.1296), half-brother of Henry III. Though known as Earl of Pembroke, William was never formally invested with the title. His son Aymer died childless in 1324 and Pembroke passed to his nearest relative, John de Hastings. Most of the subsequent owners were absentee landlords, and by 1377 the

Pembroke castle.

Pembroke: In the foreground the foundations of the gate to the inner ward are visable, with the great round keep behind.

castle was in such a poor state that Edward III ordered repairs to be carried out. The Hastings line was similarly short-lived, and in 1389 the title became extinct and Pembroke passed to the Crown. From then on the decaying fortress was granted out to various noblemen including Humphrey, Duke of Gloucester (d.1447), William, Duke of Suffolk (d.1450) and Jasper Tudor (d.1495). Even the ill-fated Anne Boleyn was briefly created Marchioness of Pembroke in 1532.

By then only some of the buildings would have been habitable, and around 1600 George Owen reported that all 'the rooffes and leades have been taken down'. Nevertheless the gutted shell was still a formidable obstacle for Parliamentarian success in the Civil War, and the Royalist garrison endured a long siege between May and July 1648. After they surrendered, the defences were slighted; sections of the town walls were knocked down and most of the towers of the outer ward blown up. For years the great ruin attracted artists and antiquarians, and Richard Fenton

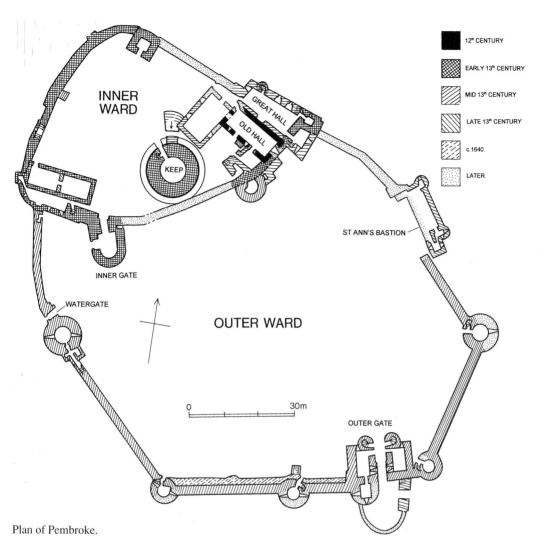

Plan of Pembroke.

■	12th CENTURY
▨	EARLY 13th CENTURY
▨	MID 13th CENTURY
▨	LATE 13th CENTURY
▨	c.1640
▦	LATER

INNER WARD

GREAT HALL

OLD HALL

KEEP

ST ANN'S BASTION

INNER GATE

WATERGATE

OUTER WARD

OUTER GATE

0   30m

considered that the '*variety of architecture, and boldness of situation for look or defence, may vie with, if not excel, any ancient structure of the kind in Wales*'. What would Fenton say today, now that the shattered walls and towers have been reconstructed?

Architecture. The castle is entered from the town along a restored D-shaped barbican which leads to the outer gatehouse. This massive structure is something of a hybrid between the simple gates of the early thirteenth century, and the more elaborate structures of the Edwardian period. There is only one flanking tower, though the adjacent Barbican Tower gave some additional

defence. At the rear of the gatehouse two newel stairs lead to spacious apartments on the upper floors (which now contain excellent displays on the history of Pembroke).

Part of the curtain wall in the outer ward has been thickened on the inside, probably in an attempt to withstand the impact of cannon fire in the Civil War. Five round flanking towers guard this side of the castle, each containing several floors of storerooms and rather basic domestic chambers. The tower immediately west of the gatehouse is the traditional birthplace of Henry VII, whose mother sheltered in Pembroke when Jasper Tudor was Earl. John Leland was shown the

105

chamber in which the happy event took place, and which had just received a commemorative coat of arms over the fireplace. This room now houses an imaginative tableau of the infant Henry with his family.

The curtain wall on the north side of the ward appears never to have been completed as intended, and the 'missing link' with the inner ward has been filled in with a low parapet and round flanking turrets, known as St Ann's Bastion.

The smaller inner ward lies at the far end of the ridge, surrounded on three sides by limestone cliffs above the Pembroke river. The remainder of the enclosure was protected on its most vulnerable side by a thick curtain wall fronted by a deep rock-cut ditch crossing the ridge from edge to edge. This wall has three flanking towers of different shape; an unusual D-shaped gatetower (now unfortunately reduced to foundations), then a round tower containing a dark dungeon at its lowest level, and finally a small square garderobe turret on the cliff edge. Near the

inner gatehouse is the watergate postern, which gave access to the riverside and is thought to mark one of the old approaches to the castle.

All the principal buildings were located within the securely defended inner ward, and include a courthouse, a vaulted hall for the garrison, and a complex group of residential apartments of various dates. Embedded within this group is a rectangular block containing a first floor hall over a low storeroom. This has Norman characteristics and may very well be the oldest surviving masonry here, dating to the time of Richard de Clare. Alongside stand the more substantial remains of the Great Hall, with its finely carved stonework contrasting with the more austere work elsewhere in the castle. This was clearly the work of William de Valence and shows more of an emphasis on domestic comfort rather than military strength; nevertheless the roofline was provided with battlements and look-out turrets at each corner. From the basement a newel stair descends to a spectacular natural

Pembroke: the gatehouse and ruined barbican.

cavern beneath the castle, with a north-facing entrance partly blocked by a massive wall. This surprising feature seems to have been incorporated into the defences at an early date, and functioned as a boathouse with easy access to the tidal river.

The crowning feature of Pembroke castle is the round keep, a five storeyed cylindrical tower 15.8m in diameter, and rising from a splayed base to a height of almost 23m. The entrance was at first floor level and was covered by a timber porch with some kind of retractable bridge. A newel stair led from the dark basement storeroom to the roof, linking all the floors, but the standard of accommodation was very basic, and only two of the rooms had fireplaces. The summit of the keep is covered by a thick stone dome with double ramparts, and on the very top of the vault the foundations of a round turret can be seen. There are holes around the outer face of the battlements indicating that the tower could be fitted out with a timber hourd, and it may be that the upper level battlements and turret simply served to support the great timbers of the conical roof. This dizzying vantage point provides an excellent bird's-eye view of the castle and town, and also of Monkton priory church, the Old Hall, and Priory Farm tower house to the south.

The Medieval town lay on the narrow ridge east of the castle, with narrow burgage plots extending back from the long single street. The townsfolk were served by two churches, and by the fifteenth century suburbs had developed in the vicinity of Monkton priory. Defensive walls with six flanking towers were built late in the thirteenth century, to guard the weaker east and south sides from attack. Barnard's Tower on the north-east corner survives remarkably intact, and seems to have been the self-contained residence of some official. There were three floors, but only one habitable chamber, and this was reached through a square forebuilding armed with a portcullis. The most unusual feature of the tower is the archaic detail which indicates that it was modelled on William Marshal's keep – could

it have been built before the rest of the town walls, functioning as an independent tower house? According to John Leland the town had three gates, of which the eastgate was *'the fairest and strongest, having afore hit a compasid Tour not rofid, in the entering wherof is a Portcolys'*. In other words, the gate was an open barbican like the better-preserved Five Arches at Tenby. Only a few fragments of the Westgate remain today.

Until recently the dating of Pembroke followed the work of the great castleologist D.J.C. King, who published an invaluable survey in 1978. King believed that virtually all of the building was the work of William Marshal between 1189 and 1219. Doubts have now been expressed about this accepted view, and while Marshal was certainly responsible for building the keep and most of the inner ward, the more ambitious defences of the outer ward clearly belong to succeeding generations. William de Valence has been put forward as a likely candidate, but although the sheer size of the ward is typical of the Edwardian period, the more basic details (particularly the ineffective arrowslits) would be more at home in the first half of the thirteenth century. The Marshal heirs had sufficient time to build such an enclosure before their line came to an end in 1245, and they carried out similar large-scale works at Chepstow and Usk. Valence was certainly responsible for the more refined details of the Great Hall and adjoining buildings, and St Ann's Bastion.

In the 1880s the castle enthusiast J. R. Cobb carried out certain repairs and excavated the foundations of some of the inner ward buildings. In 1928 Sir Ivor Philipps acquired Pembroke and went even further than Cobb, restoring many lost features and completely re-building the walls and towers shattered in the Civil War.

Refs: Gerald / Leland / AC 1978, 1982 / Soulsby / Fort 1991.

PICTON (SN 011 134)

History. Picton Castle is one of the finest stately homes in west Wales, and has remained in continuous occupation since it was built around 1300. Richard Fenton praised Picton as a building *'never forfeited, never deserted, never vacant, that never knew a melancholy blank in its want of a master, from whose walls hospitality was never exiled'*.

There are two versions of the origin of the castle; one claims that a nearby motte was built by William de Picton at the close of the eleventh century, and the entire estate subsequently passed via the Picton heiress to Sir John Wogan of Wiston. The other version holds that the land belonged to Wizo the Fleming and that his descendants, the Wogans, established Picton to replace the older castle at Wiston. However, most authorities accept that the existing castle was built by Sir John, Chief Justiciary of Ireland between 1298 and 1309.

The Wogans held Picton until the estate passed to the Dwnns of Kidwelly in the fifteenth century. On the death of Henry Dwnn in 1469, his daughter married Thomas ap Philip, and Picton has remained with descendants of the Philipps family ever since. In 1405 Owain Glyndŵr's French mercenaries sacked 'Picot' castle after failing to take Haverfordwest, and the only other recorded attack occurred in 1645 when Sir Richard Philipps held the castle for the king. Picton was captured after Sir Richard's infant son was snatched out of the arms of a nursemaid, who incautiously leant out of the window to take a message from a soldier. The baby was held to ransom and Sir Richard gave up the castle. However, the Parliamentarian commander felt so ashamed of his actions that he allowed the building to remain intact.

The subsequent history of Picton has less relevance here, as it devolved into a fine country seat, with many alterations being carried out, and a general softening up of the war-like features. The gardens and craft shop are open during the summer months, and there are guided tours of the castle on certain days.

Architecture. Given its long transformation into a stately home, it comes as no surprise to find that Picton has few surviving Medieval features within the massively thick walls. There are some blocked early windows in the gatehouse, and the vaulted undercroft

Picton castle.

beneath the hall is largely intact; otherwise the interior decor originates from the re-furbishments carried out in the eighteenth and nineteenth centuries.

From the outside Picton resembles a typical Edwardian enclosure castle with flanking towers on the corners (like Chirk in north Wales), but in fact it is a solid block, and could be better classed as a tower house rather than a true castle. The plan features a two storeyed rectangular hall, with three storeyed round towers on four corners, and a lost D-shaped tower at the narrower west end. Squeezed in between the towers at the east end of the hall is a little twin-towered gatehouse which rises higher than the remaining roofline. The gate was originally entered at ground level, and led to a straight flight of stairs rising to the hall. In the eighteenth century the entrance was modified and a new access provided at first floor level. The closest British counterpart to Picton is Nunney (Somerset), but the towers at Carlow, Ferns and Lea in Ireland probably influenced Sir John's choice of design.

Two drawings exist which show the appearance of Picton prior to refurbishment, and the earliest is dated 1684 by Thomas Dineley. This crude sketch depicts the gatehouse and two of the flanking towers, topped by a corbelled parapet of equal height. Above the entrance a decorative plaque is shown, which probably bore a coat of arms. The castle stands within a rectangular enclosure surrounded by a low battlemented wall of dubious strength. The gate is clearly a Renaissance doorway, and the outer enclosure may well be just a boundary wall of post-Medieval date. Behind the castle the peaked roof of a large building (perhaps a chapel?) can be seen. By the time the Buck brothers drew Picton in 1740 the outer enclosure had vanished and the overall view is closer to what survives today. The most interesting features are the perpendicular windows of the hall, which date to the fifteenth century, and suggest that the Dwnns refurbished the building after Glyndŵr's attack.

Refs: RCAHM 1925 / AJ 1962 / King / Jones.

TENBY (SN 138 005)

History. '*Tinbigh Town stondith on a main Rokke, but not veri hy, and the Severn se so gulfeth in about hit, that at the ful se, almost the thirde part of the toune is inclosid with water*'. John Leland's archaic description of Tenby in the late 1530s highlights the defensive advantages of the rocky headland as a settlement site. Prehistoric and Roman finds have been made here, and the unknown bard of a ninth or tenth century poem praised the hospitality of the Welsh lord of this '*fine fortress on the broad ocean*'.

However, the impetus for the growth of a permanent settlement was provided by the Norman invasion in the late eleventh century. A castle must have been established here soon after the founding of Pembroke in 1093, for there exist documents referring to the town church around 1100. In 1151 Cadell ap Gruffudd was attacked and crippled by some soldiers from Tenby, and in revenge his brothers Maredudd and Rhys stormed the castle at night and massacred the garrison. Maelgwn ap Rhys burnt the town in 1187, and in 1260 Llywelyn ap Gruffudd repeated the destruction.

Work on re-building the town and castle defences was probably initiated by the erstwhile Earl of Pembroke, William de Valence, after this attack. The first recorded murage grant is dated 1328 and this allowed the townsfolk to levy tolls on imported merchandise to pay for the building works. A later earl, Jasper Tudor, issued another charter in 1457 with the specific clause to make the walls 1.8m wide '*so that men may be able to perambulate and circulate upon the said walls for its defence*'. The strength of these outer defences is such that Tenby alone, of all the towns in west Wales, retains an almost intact circuit.

The town flourished and grew throughout the later Middle Ages and the Elizabethan period, and many fine buildings survive from this time. Others have unfortunately been lost through subsequent decline and modern re-building. Although the town walls were

The castle gate and barbican, Tenby.

periodically repaired and patched up (particularly during the Armada scare of 1588), the rather insignificant castle appears to have decayed fairly early. Nevertheless, the town withstood an attack by Owain Glyndŵr in 1405, and changed hands several times during the Civil War; on one occasion the battered castle was caught in an artillery bombardment from land and sea. In more recent times a museum has been built within one of the ruined buildings on the headland.

The Five Arches gate, Tenby.

Architecture. The town walls are now the most impressive part of the Medieval defences and deserve to be examined first. They survive virtually intact apart from the missing north gate. A recent study of the masonry has shown that the first phase (possibly early thirteenth century) consisted of a thin, rather low wall, apparently fronting an earlier earth bank with an outer ditch. Only two of the surviving six flanking towers belong to this phase, the others being added at later dates when the wall was also heightened and thickened to provide a continuous walkway.

Whether the wall ever enclosed the side of the town facing the sea is open to debate; stretches of early masonry have been recorded along the clifftops, but the sheer drop would have made artificial defence superfluous and the circuit was probably never completed. There was, however, a wall running from the north cliff down to the harbour, where the Medieval chapel of St Julian stood.

John Leland recorded that each of the four gates into the town had a portcullis and that the north, or Carmarthen Gate, was '*the most semliest, as circulid without, with an embatelid but open rofid tower'*. In fact, Leland seems to be describing the south gate, which is today better known as the Five Arches. The name is highly misleading since four of the arches are just arrowslits that were knocked through in the last century (and the town planners even tried to demolish the gate in its entirety!). The gate takes the form of a simple entrance arch through the wall, defended by a D-shaped barbican with a single gate closed by wooden doors and a portcullis. The portcullis was originally worked from the battlements, but when the walls were raised the open walkway became a vaulted gallery. Barbicans of this type are fairly uncommon, but examples are known from Pembroke, Goodrich (Herefordshire) and the Tower of London.

The castle lies below the town on a headland jutting into the sea, a setting which closely parallels the better known Tintagel in Cornwall. Given the unusual topography of the site, we cannot be sure if a typical motte or ringwork was built here, and so the appearance of twelfth century Tenby castle is unknown. Today the headland is covered with scattered fragments of towers and walls of various periods, and it is clear that the uneven and irregular site could never have allowed a coherent plan. There was no complete circuit, just a group of buildings linked by a few short stretches of curtain walls, and the builders relied much on the protection offered by the sea cliffs.

The solitary gatehouse is a simple and unambitious square tower defended by a portcullis, with a little barbican reminiscent of the Five Arches. On the east side of the gate stood a two storeyed building that probably contained a hall on the first floor, while over on the north side of the headland is a more ruinous building that might have been a barn or store.

The town museum has been built within the shell of a large two storeyed block with a corbelled parapet, but no other early features survive inside. There are foundations of probable Medieval buildings adjoining the museum, and on the highest part of the hill stands the mis-named 'keep'. This was never a residential building and consists of a small round turret with an added stairway; its size and location suggests it functioned as a beacon or look-out, and might even have been a re-used windmill.

Refs: Brut / Leland / Soulsby / AC 1993 / AJ 1962.

WISTON (SN 023 182)

History. Wiston is arguably the finest earthwork castle in Dyfed, and recent conservation work by CADW has preserved the crumbling masonry defences and removed the dense covering of undergrowth that formerly shrouded the site. Here the visitor can see all the salient features of a motte and bailey, as well as the first stages of a reconstruction in stone that, had it been carried to completion, would have turned the twelfth century frontier fortress into a major Medieval stronghold.

Wiston was founded in the early years of the twelfth century by one of the Flemish colonists King Henry I encouraged to settle in this area. Their leader was Wizo, who gave his name to the castle and adjoining settlement. Wizo's castle was a substantial structure, and when a Welsh army led by Cadell, Maredudd and Rhys ap Gruffudd besieged it in 1147 they were met with initial failure. The triumvirate even had to employ the resources of their enemy, Hywel ap Owain Gwynedd, before Wiston was taken *'with great toil and conflict'*. In 1193 Hywel Sais gained entry to the castle *'by treachery'* and imprisoned Philip fitz Wizo and his family; but the Welsh triumph was short-lived, and within a few years the English were back in control.

Llywelyn Fawr burnt the castle and town on his violent crusade through west Wales in 1220, and this marks the last appearance of Wiston in the Chronicles. However, finds from recent excavations have indicated that the castle was still occupied in the late

The arched entrance to the shell-keep at Wiston.

fourteenth century, by which time the estate had passed to the Wogans of nearby Picton. A minor branch of this influential and widespread family built a manor house beside the castle, and this is now represented by a farmhouse. The neglected fortress was subsequently used as an ornamental feature in a landscaped park.

Architecture. Perhaps the most striking feature of Wiston castle is the scale of the surviving earthworks; the motte itself is 9.2m high, with a summit diameter of 16m, and the adjoining bailey occupies an area of about 2.5 acres. It may be that the large enclosure is an Iron Age hillfort re-used by the Flemish settlers, but given the exceptional size of the motte, then the bailey could also be contemporary and could reflect the scale and ambition of Wizo's colony.

The motte straddles the north side of the bailey rampart, and is crowned with a stone shell-keep, 12m internal diameter, with walls now standing up to 3.6m high. The multi-

sided building has weathered badly and parts have fallen, but the simple entrance gate is intact. Originally there would have been timber lean-to buildings ranged against the inner wall, but recent excavations by the Dyfed Archaeological Trust have revealed the footings of a later cross-wall forming part of a two storeyed building occupying the northern half of the enclosure. Finds from the dig included pieces of roofing tiles and window glass. At a later date the wall was thickened on the inside, and it is possible that the keep was eventually roofed over forming, in effect, a solid, squat tower.

The date of the stonework is not known for certain, and it has been suggested that the keep was built in the 1220s when Henry III ordered William Marshal II to strengthen the local castles after Llywelyn's raid. An earlier date is equally plausible on architectural grounds, and it is tempting to see the building of the keep as a belated safety measure after Hywel's audacious raid in 1193. There is no sign that the large bailey was ever walled in stone, but the strong bank and outer ditch made formidable defences even by the standards of the early thirteenth century. The enclosure probably housed the initial settlement and various ancillary buildings, including (no doubt) a large hall and solar for the lord and his family, to supplement the cramped accommodation within the keep.

Refs: Brut / RCAHM 1925 / DAT / CADW.

TOWER HOUSES, FORTIFIED MANORS & DEFENSIBLE HOMES

Landowners and wealthy merchants lacking the resources and social standing to build castles, nevertheless felt the need to protect their homes with some form of defence, and so built fortified manors and tower houses. The former often resemble small castles, with ditches, curtain walls and a few towers (such as Newhouse, Roche and Upton), though the defensive strength is much slighter than the real thing. Far more plentiful in west Wales are tower houses and what might be termed 'defensible homes'. Indeed, south Pembrokeshire has the largest concentration outside Scotland and the north of England, where such buildings were the norm from the late Middle Ages to the seventeenth century.

The reasons for this are not easy to identify, since Pembrokeshire was a relatively peaceful part of the country, firmly Anglicised since the twelfth century, and in no way a 'front-line' territory. In any case, the little towers dotted around the countryside could never have offered a serious obstacle to an attacking force. Were they therefore just protection against pirates and roving brigands? Given the long use of the Milford Haven waterway as a navigable route penetrating deep inland, there may be some truth in this supposition. Glyndŵr's French mercenaries came ashore at Milford in 1405, so too did Henry Tudor's army in 1485. The threat of a French invasion prompted Henry VIII to build artillery forts at Dale and Angle, in a rather forlorn attempt to guard the entrance to the Haven.

However, the surviving evidence suggests that most towers formed only one part of a larger undefended house, and that prestige (as much as peace of mind) was an important factor in their construction.

Another reason to explain the existence of such a large number, is the long tradition of building in stone in Pembrokeshire (in contrast to Montgomeryshire, for instance, where timber-framed houses predominate). As far back as 1603, George Owen noted that *'most castles and houses of any account were built with vaults very strongly and substantially wrought'.* Many domestic buildings have a vaulted undercroft with the hall and private chambers on the first floor. Such a strong and fireproof building would therefore only require narrow windows and a first floor entrance (reached by a ladder) to be capable of limited defence. Houses such as Carswell, Flimston, Scotsborough and Kingston belong to this category; they may look like ordinary homes, but have features that provide some protection against casual attack. They have close counterparts in the 'bastles' of the Scottish border region. A further step up the defensive ladder would be the construction of a rooftop wall-walk and battlements, reached by a narrow stair, for instance Bonville's Court, Caldey Priory, Eastington, Priory Farm and Roch. Of all the Pembrokeshire tower houses, pride of place goes to the very Scottish-looking Old Rectory at Angle, a remarkable building aptly described by the great castleologist D. J. C. King, as 'a doll's house'!

These small buildings have left little mark on history because they were never substantial enough to play any role in national (or even local) affairs. Dating them can be a problem too, for there is usually little architectural evidence to point the way. Eastington, Roch and Newhouse are all likely to belong to the fourteenth century, and others such as Caldey Priory and Priory Farm have features that claim a late-Medieval date. However, some of the smaller houses like Carswell, Kingston and Scotsborough, appear to be much later in date, perhaps even sixteenth century.

Most of the sites included in the following gazetteer are privately owned and there is no public access. Those marked with an asterisk can be seen from nearby roads and paths, and may be visited with prior consent from the landowner.

ANGLE (SM 866 029)*

'*To the north of . . . the church-yard are the remains of a considerable building with a square tower, very picturesque, covered with ivy, called the Castle . . . and now converted into an inn called the Castle Inn*'. Since Fenton published that description in c1811, much of the old masonry has been removed, and the tower – more commonly known as the Old Rectory – is all that survives. Whether it was ever used as such is open to debate. Originally a stone-lined moat enclosed three sides of a rectangular platform bordering a tidal creek, with square towers at the north-east and south-west corners. Only the latter remains today along with one arm of the moat, and all other buildings on the platform appear to be modern. Associated with the manor is a ruined stone dovecote in the fields just to the north.

The little tower is a most remarkable structure, quite unique in south Wales, and very similar to the pele-towers of Ireland and Scotland. There are three habitable rooms above a vaulted basement just over 3m square, and living conditions must have been intolerably cramped. All rooms have fireplaces and small, unglazed windows, and there was a garderobe on the first floor. The only entrance was at this level, and seems to have been reached by a drawbridge. There are also indications in the external stonework of a possible forebuilding or porch. Just above the door the rooflines of later buildings constructed against this side of the tower after it had outlived its usefulness for defence can be seen.

The most distinctive feature of the Angle tower is the row of massive corbels around the rooftop, which originally supported a machicolated parapet. The accompanying reconstruction drawing shows how the battlements may have looked originally, though it is possible that the corbels actually supported a more elaborate timber hourd. Such parapets are a distinctive feature of the later Middle Ages and close parallels can be seen at Nunney (Somerset) and Ceasar's Tower (Warwick), both dating from the late fourteenth century. According to Fenton the tower was built by Robert de Shirburn (or Sherbourne) in the reign of Edward III (1327-77). The Shirburns had been granted lands here in the late thirteenth century by the lord of the manor, Philip de Angulo, and appeared to have retained the property until the fifteenth century. *Since the above was written, the tower house has been consolidated and public access is allowed.*

The Old Rectory, Angle.

114

Angle: A cutaway view through the fourteenth century tower house. The cramped tower was elaborately defended by a drawbridge and possibly a porch or forebuilding, with a machicolated parapet around the top (it is possible that the battlements were timber, not stone, as shown).

There is one other building worth noting in the little village; behind the Post Office stand the remains of a first floor hall, misleadingly known as a 'Castle' or 'Nunnery'. It originally had a massive timber floor instead of the usual vault, but the thick walls and narrow ground floor windows hint at some defensive considerations. Unfortunately too little of the building survives for the complete plan to be recovered. *Refs: Fenton / AC 1867, 1868 / CS / HWC / Jones / DAT / H. Owen.*

BONVILLE'S COURT (SN 125 052)

This site disappeared from the landscape in the early years of this century, a victim of the little-known coal mining industry of south Pembrokeshire. Nevertheless, it is possible to make a tolerably accurate reconstruction of the building, thanks to notes and illustrations published by E. L. Barnwell in the 1860s.

The Bonville family moved from the west country, and Nicholas, the reputed builder, was holding land here in the early fourteenth century. The house comprised a ground floor hall, with a two storeyed tower at the solar end (virtually identical in plan to Eastington). Barnwell thought (incorrectly) that the hall was an addition to the free-standing tower. Two arched doorways led into vaulted ground floor rooms, and a stair in one chamber led up to the first floor. This level was occupied by a single large room with a vaulted roof, and the stair climbed to an upper chamber, perhaps containing a garderobe. Barnwell also noted the remains of a walled courtyard surrounding the house.

Later owners of Bonville's Court evidently increased the accommodation, for it was assessed as having seven hearths in the Hearth Tax returns of 1670. By the end of the nineteenth century the building had fallen into decay and was used as colliery workrooms, eventually being buried under a waste tip.
Refs: AC 1867, 1868.

CALDEY PRIORY (SS 141 962)*

The old priory on Caldey Island was founded in the early twelfth century as a dependent cell of St Dogmael's Abbey, near Cardigan. The small community here was isolated and remote, and sometime in the fourteenth century a tower house was added at one end of the existing cloister range, to offer some degree of protection against the risk of a pirate raid. The principal function of the tower was just to provide the prior with a prestigious and fairly secure residence. At the Dissolution of the Monasteries in 1536 the property was seized by the king, and then sold off to John Bradshaw of Presteigne. The tenant farmers running the estate were responsible for constucting most of the surviving buildings adjoining the old church and tower.

The Prior's Tower stands at the north end of the charming little cloister and can easily be detected by its battlemented parapet. There is only a single living room inside, with a fireplace and garderobe, which occupies the first floor above a vaulted storeroom. The entrance was at this level and was reached by an external wooden stair (the outlines of the blocked doorway can be seen in the west wall). A destroyed stair turret in one corner led up to the battlements. Through the empty windows of the tower it is possible to glimpse the sturdy timbers of an intact late-Medieval roof – a rare surviving feature in buildings of this type.
Refs: AC 1908 / DAT / HWC.

CARSWELL (SN 098 010)*

West of Tenby the marshy Ritec valley (once an inlet of the sea) winds inland for a distance of 4km to St Florence. Along the sides of the valley are several ruined buildings which have a notable element of defence in their construction (see also Scotsborough).

The defensible house at Carswell.

The best-preserved is at Carswell farm, now in the care of CADW, and is accessible to the public. The little building contains only two rooms; a vaulted ground floor kitchen, and an upper dwelling chamber measuring just 5m square. Fireplaces on both floors are served by a huge chimney stack in the end wall. There was no communication between rooms, and the only access to the first floor was by means of a removable ladder-stair. A similar building (not accessible) stands on the other side of the farmyard. The placename is recorded as far back as the early fourteenth century, but on architectural grounds, the little house is probably not much older than c1500. A Phyllyp Nicholl is recorded as living here in 1543.

Only 1km away at West Tarr is another pair of vaulted buildings (not yet open to the public), which stand on sloping ground and are less obviously designed for defence. The main building has the usual ladder-stair entry, and the single upper chamber also has a vaulted roof. Carswell and West Tarr lie just off a minor road from St Florence to Penally. *Refs: CADW / Jones.*

DALE (SM 806 058)*

Dale was an outlying manor of the barony of Walwyn's Castle, but while the principal stronghold never evolved beyond a simple earthwork fort, Dale has grown into a rambling battlemented mansion. It lies in a quiet valley on the coast and, although outwardly of nineteenth century date, incorporates the remains of Medieval vaulted rooms. Unfortunately, not enough of the plan survives to indicate what form the original building took, or whether it was a castle or just a fortified manor.

The de Vales held the property from the twelfth to the beginning of the fourteenth century, and in 1293 Robert de Vale received a grant to hold a weekly market and an annual fair here. On his death, the estate was split up among various heiresses, and Dale subsequently passed to the Walters family. One of the more famous members of this clan was Lucy, mistress of Charles II and mother of his illegitimate son, the Duke of Monmouth. Her brother, Richard Walter, sold Dale in 1669 and the property was later acquired by the Lloyd-Philipps family, who carried out extensive re-building work, and still hold the castle to this day. *Refs: Jones / Miles.*

EASTINGTON (SM 901 024)*

Eastington tower house lies alongside a country lane beyond Rhoscrowther church, a tranquil setting marred only by the huge oil refinery on the hillside above. The interior is currently inaccessible, but the exterior can be seen from the road.

Eastington was the home of the Perrot family until the main seat was transferred to Haroldston near Haverfordwest, in the sixteenth century; with the house then passing to the Philipps' and then the Meres. The latter family built a large new house adjoining the upper end of the Medieval building, which then declined in importance. The Perrot house was probably built in the fourteenth century and consists of a first floor

117

Eastington: This cutaway shows the main first floor chamber and the stone steps (which replaced an original wooden stair). Few traces now remain of the building (probably a hall) shown on the right.

hall with a dark vaulted undercroft, and a small turret containing garderobes. This plan is repeated (with minor variations) all through south Pembrokeshire – but the Perrots went one step further. They added battlements around the roof, and made the first floor entrance accessible only by a wooden ladder (this was subsequently replaced by a stone stair).

Against the outer face of the house the outlines of a demolished single storey building can be seen, which some authorities think is an addition but is more likely to be original. This lost building was probably a hall, and the surviving tower house was just the fortified solar.

Refs: RCAHM 1925 / HWC / Jones.

FLIMSTON (SR 923 956)*

Far out on the lonely expanse of the Castlemartin firing range is a sprawling farmstead long deserted and ruinous. Incorporated within the outwardly modern-looking house is a Medieval building consisting of a ground floor hall, with a solar wing above a vaulted undercroft. The presence of two blocked first floor doorways suggests that the solar wing was only accessible by an outside stair, and may have been a free-standing block originally. A similar arrangement has been detected at nearby Pricaston, another deserted farmstead on the range. *Refs: HWC.*

KINGSTON FARM (SR 994 993)

Adjoining the end of a range of modern farm buildings is a tiny two storeyed tower house, very similar to those at Carswell and West Tarr. The vaulted ground floor measures only 2.6m by 3.7m and the upper chamber (still accessible only by ladder) is hardly any larger. The gable chimney stack has been cut down in recent times. There are no signs of any other early buildings at the farm, and yet it seems inconceivable that this little dwelling is all there ever was here. There is no conclusive evidence to date the building, but the style of the upper window (shown in the reconstruction drawing) would not be incompatible with a sixteenth century date. *Refs: HWC.*

A reconstruction of the little tower at Kingston.

NEWHOUSE (SN 072 136)

This neglected and poorly documented site lies deep in a tangled forest on the edge of Canaston Woods. The placename is recorded as *Novadomus* in 1357, and by 1609 it had acquired a second title, *'Newehouse alias Red Castle'*. In the past Newhouse has been classed as a moated site or 'stronghouse' – names which belittle its defensive capabilities, for the rock-cut ditches alone are more than 4m deep.

All that now remains above ground is a two storey hall block, but the surrounding rectangular courtyard is enclosed by a strong bank containing much tumbled stone, and a heap of rubble at the south-west corner appears to mark the remains of a round tower. The gatehouse probably stood at the opposite south-east corner, but this side has been damaged by a later causeway built to provide easy access across the ditch.

All timberwork within the building has decayed away and so the exact layout is uncertain. The hall lay on the first floor originally and was reached by an external wooden stair; an additional newel stair in one corner led to the basement and the rooftop. There is no sign of an original fireplace, and so the hall must have been warmed by a hearth set on a stone platform rising from the ground floor (this method of supporting a hearth on a timber floor was also used at Carreg Cennen and Dryslwyn).

Dating the building is a bit of a problem, since there are no obvious indications of age. Given the rather basic features and absence of garderobes, fireplaces, and glazed windows, then a date in the late thirteenth or early fourteenth century is likely. Certainly the spartan hall was useless for the needs of later owners, and at some time in the sixteenth or seventeenth century, a major refit was carried out. A third of the building was disused and cut off by a cross-wall provided with multiple fireplaces, and an extra floor put in at attic level.

The later history of Newhouse is as obscure as its beginning; it was held by the Barlow family of Slebech, and there is a tradition that it was inhabited by a widow of a certain Colonel Thomas, killed in the battle of St Fagans in 1648. By the time Fenton passed through the area, Newhouse was in ruins and any memory of its military origin was lost. *Refs: Fenton / AC 1922 /Charles.*

Newhouse: This cutaway reconstruction shows the hall block as it might have appeared soon after completion. The room must have been warmed by a central hearth, and it is likely that timber partitions divided up the interior. The doorway that can just be glimpsed in the far corner appears to have led out onto the vanished curtain wall.

PRIORY FARM (SM 978 014)*

Hidden behind the more obviously ancient Monkton Priory and Old Hall, is an outwardly modernised building that incorporates the remains of a late-Medieval tower house. The house consists of a rectangular block containing a ground floor store and an upper hall originally reached by an arched doorway on the first floor (now converted into a window). On one side of the hall is a three storeyed square tower with a vaulted undercroft. The battlements have been removed and replaced with attic rooms, and there is no sign of an early stairway to the roof. Priory Farm must have been connected with the adjacent Benedictine priory, and was perhaps the defended residence of the prior (as at Caldey). A stone dovecote survives in the adjacent fields.
Refs: HWC / CS.

ROCH CASTLE (SM 880 212)*

Legend has it that Adam de la Roche (or Rupe) built this castle on a high rock to foil a prophecy that he would die by an adder's bite. Destiny however, could not be averted and the fatal snake was unwittingly brought into his lofty room hidden in a bundle of firewood. The builders had more mundane reasons for siting a castle here - not only did the volcanic outcrop provide a secure foundation against undermining, but from the top the countryside for miles around could be kept under surveillance.

Roch was probably established in the early twelfth century by an Anglo-Norman settler, whose descendants took their name from this natural geological feature. The historical Adam de la Roche founded Pill priory near Milford Haven around 1200, and the lordship was held by this family until the death of Thomas c1413. The estate was conveyed by his two heiresses to Lord Ferrers and Sir George Longueville, and was jointly held until it was sold in 1601 to a local landowner, William Walter. During the Civil War the castle changed hands twice and may have been burnt down. The building was certainly ruinous for centuries before it was purchased in 1899 by John Philipps, First Viscount St Davids, and completely restored. The shattered walls were re-built, new floors, roofs and windows were put in, and additional accommodation was provided by inserting an extra floor in the roof space.

On architectural grounds, Roch was constructed around 1300, probably by John de la Roche (d.1314), and consists of a three storeyed tower of D-shaped plan. The entrance lay above basement level originally and must have been reached by a timber stair (and drawbridge?). Within, the two upper floors originally contained single large residential apartments, with little vaulted chambers housed in a square turret projecting from the curved front of the tower. Perhaps the main rooms were divided by timber partitions originally, but all existing internal walls are modern. If there were any other buildings here, none have survived. On the south side of the castle the earthwork remains of a narrow bailey platform curving around the base of the rock can be seen, which probably formed part of the original twelfth century defences. Roch is still privately owned, but can be hired for use as a holiday home. *Refs: Fenton / King / Miles / H.Owen.*

Roch Castle.

ROCHE CASTLE (SN 294 102)*

Although called such, Roche is not a true castle, but a moated manor defended by masonry walls - a feature shared by only two other sites in Wales. Little is known of its history; it was probably held by the de la Rupe family in the mid thirteenth century, and was granted to Sir John Perrot in 1575. Much of the structure was robbed for building materials in the seventeenth century, and more recently the site has been encroached on by modern bungalows.

The moat lies in a shallow valley west of Laugharne, and can just be seen from the A4066. The site consists of an irregular platform surrounded by a shallow ditch that was probably once filled with water from the adjacent stream. Several buildings have been detected within the courtyard, but all that remains above ground is a short length of ivy-covered masonry forming part of a hall block with a vaulted undercroft, and rounded turrets on two corners. One of the turrets contained a newel stair. *Refs: CA vol IX.*

SANDYHAVEN (SM 851 076)*

Although this large country house may look like a typical castellated construction of the eighteenth and nineteenth centuries, it actually embodies the remains of a Medieval tower house. Despite subsequent alterations it is still possible to detect an early building of T-shape plan (very similar to Eastington), consisting of a three storeyed tower with an adjoining hall block. The hall presumably lay on the first floor above a vaulted undercroft, but the upper parts of the building have been considerably modernised. At some point in the seventeenth century the tower was heightened and an extra wing added to one side. Sandyhaven is a private residence, but the exterior can be seen from a minor road east of St Ishmael's. *Refs: NMR.*

SCOTSBOROUGH HOUSE (SN 117 011)*

Home to a branch of the Perrots of Eastington from the early fifteenth to the late sixteenth centuries. One wing of this Medieval house has a vaulted undercroft with a first floor solar, and an adjoining vaulted turret. There are no battlements, but all the original windows (even on the first floor) are narrow loopholes, hinting at some defensive capability. *Refs: AC 1906 / AW 1990.*

SISTER'S HOUSE (SN 033 135)

The tangled ruin of Sister's House on the banks of the Cleddau near Minwear, has long puzzled historians, on account of the ecclesiastical sounding placename. In all likelihood it was just a large secular mansion (like Boulston). There is no evidence of any fortifications here, but two small defensible houses of the Carswell type survive fairly intact beside the ruined hall. They have gable fireplaces and vaulted undercrofts, but since the whole site is so badly preserved it is not clear if they were free-standing or formed part of a larger building. *Refs: HWC / NMR.*

UPPER LAMPHEY PARK (SN 025 012)*

This little tower house was only discovered in 1994, and yet it appears as a tiny detail in a Buck engraving of 1740! There, it is shown resembling a church tower between two buildings, one of which is undoubtedly the large barn that still adjoins the south side. The other structure has long since vanished, but it is marked by a row of corbels on the north side of the tower, indicating that it was a two storeyed building perhaps with a first floor hall.

The tower is now roofless and ruined, and contains single rooms on two floors. It lacks the usual vaulted undercroft, but the little stair turret is a typical feature. The newel stair appears to have risen to either a third floor, or vanished battlements. The tower can be seen from a public footpath at Upper Lamphey Park farm, just north-east of the village. *Refs: Austin.*

UPTON (SN 020 047)*

From the outside Upton appears to be a large and rambling Medieval building with round towers, battlements, and a corbelled roofline; but in fact only a small part of the castle is old. Most of the existing structure was built in Gothic style in the early nineteenth century. The original part is a much-altered oblong block with round turrets on two of the outward facing corners. There are now three floors inside, but probably there were only two at first, with the hall on the uppermost. In one corner of the hall there is a newel stair, and in the other, one of a pair of small turrets flanking a vaulted gateway. This probably led into a central courtyard. The only other early masonry here is a vaulted undercroft embedded in the rear wing of the house.

Upton is believed to have been built in the fourteenth century by the Malefants, some of whom rest in peace beneath fine stone effigies in the adjacent chapel. In the fifteenth century the manor passed to Owain, son of Gruffudd ap Nicholas of Dinefwr, who married the Malefant heiress. Their descendants styled themselves Bowen, and held the estate until 1706, producing several high sheriffs along the way. The castle was said to be in ruins by 1810, but by the 1830s the present mansion had been built around the older remains. It is still a private residence, although the grounds and chapel can be visited in the summer, and can be reached via a signposted road from the A477. *Refs: CS / Jones / NMR.*

POSSIBLE SITES
(not marked on map)

BOULSTON (SM 982 123)

Within the ruins of the Elizabethan mansion at Boulston (home to a branch of the Wogans of Picton) are the remains of a substantial Medieval first floor hall. Only excavation will recover the full plan, but a vaulted undercroft survives, and the thick walls suggest that the original building had some defensive capabilities. *Refs: RCAHM 1925 / AW 1990.*

CAREW RECTORY (SN 044 027)

The present rectory just west of Carew Cheriton church incorporates a three storeyed square tower with a flanking stair turret, and a corbelled parapet. It is used as the entrance to the house, and may have been just a gatehouse to a larger (lost) mansion rather than a true tower house. Fenton also noted the remains of *'a very high and embattled wall'*. *Refs: Fenton / HWC.*

CRESWELL CASTLE (SN 048 071)

A mock-Medieval castle built by Bishop Barlow of St Davids in the early sixteenth century beside the Creswell river. There is a rectangular courtyard with round corner turrets, but despite the battlements and towers this was just a mansion dressed up as a feudal stronghold. *Refs: Fenton / RCAHM 1925.*

GREEN CASTLE (SN 396 166)

Also known as Castell Moel, this impressive ruin stands on a ridge beside the B4312 south of Carmarthen. The main building is a sixteenth century first floor hall, with an adjoining multi-storeyed stair turret. Although an engraving of 1740 shows a battlemented wall, the remains are clearly undefended, and formed part of a manor house belonging to the Rede family. *Refs: RCAHM 1917.*

QUAY ST, HAVERFORDWEST (SM 954 155)

A possible tower house in Quay St was dismantled in 1983 and removed to the Museum of Welsh Life at St Fagans, where it will be re-built in the next few years. The building is similar to Carswell, with a vaulted ground floor kitchen, and a first floor chamber reached by an external stair. However, there are few signs of defensive pretensions, and the house stood in a very vulnerable position overlooked by higher ground. *Refs: MWL / HWC.*

ST BRIDE'S CASTLE (SM 804 107)

Alongside a wooded footpath to St Bride's Castle (a nineteenth century house) is a group of ruined buildings, including a tall, three storeyed tower-like structure. There are several door and window openings in the ivy-covered walls, and this might be a much-altered tower house.

STACKPOLE COURT (SR 977 961)

The huge mansion of the Cawdor family was demolished in 1962, and though outwardly of eighteenth century date, it incorporated much older fabric. The vaulted cellars were Medieval and possibly formed part of a fortified building, since the Court was garrisoned in the Civil War.

TOWY CASTLE (SN 405 143)

A doubtful site. Medieval pottery and stonework has been ploughed up at this hilltop site south of Carmarthen.

Placename evidence or documentary sources suggest that castles or fortified houses may have existed at the following sites:
Abermarlais (SN 692 295)
Allt-y-gaer (SN 572 209)
Castell Maelgwyn (SN 214 436)
Castell Myn (SN 348 545)
Cilsant (SN 260 239)
Goedmor (SN 195 435)
Lawrenny (SN 015 067)
Llyswen (SN 460 618)
Mynydd Morvil (SN 033 315)
Peithyll (SN 631 826)

GLOSSARY

Bailey — Another name for the ward, or courtyard of a castle.

Barbican — A fortified extension of a gateway.

Bastion — A flanking projection or turret designed to give defenders a better field of fire beyond the walls.

Burgage — Freehold property in a Medieval town. Burgage plots usually take the form of narrow strips of land extending back from the street.

Buttery — A storehouse, mainly for drinks.

Buttress — A masonry projection designed to support and strengthen a wall.

Corbel — A small projecting stone bracket, supporting beams, roof trusses etc. Where the battlements or roof are carried on a row of corbels, this is known as a corbel-table.

Counterscarp — The rampart or bank along the outer edge of a ditch, giving additional depth to the earthworks.

Curtain wall — The high wall enclosing the bailey, linking up towers etc.

Dovecot — A structure designed to house pigeons, usually a pepperpot-shaped building with nesting holes on the inner walls.

Garderobe — A Medieval euphemism for privy or latrine.

Hourd — A wooden fighting platform projecting from the tops of walls and towers, usually erected as a temporary measure.

Intra-mural — Means 'within the walls', and can refer to passages, stairs, chambers etc, constructed within the thickness of the walls.

Iron Age fort — Earthwork fortifications of the pre-Roman Iron Age (c500 BC - first century AD). Often confusingly designated as 'castles' on OS maps.

Keep — The 'Donjon' or great tower of a castle.

Loop-hole — A small, vertical slit in the walls to allow light/ventilation, and for use by archers.

Moat — Water-filled ditch surrounding a castle; alternatively a manorial residence enclosed by ditches (basically a small island). The latter is not a castle, but sometimes had some defensive capabilities.

Motte — An earth and timber castle formed of a large mound, topped with a wooden palisade and tower.

Machicolation — An opening between large corbels through which missiles could be dropped on attackers at the base of a wall/tower.

Multiangular — A tower with multiple sides e.g. of hexagonal or pentagonal plan.

Mullion — The vertical dividing bar of a window.

Newel stair — Spiral stairs winding around a central post (newel).

Oriel — A projection from the walls of a building, usually containing a large window and seats.

Palisade — A timber fence or stockade, usually built along the top of a bank or mound.

Portcullis — An iron-clad wooden grill which descended in front of the entry doors in a gatehouse.

Postern — Or sally port, is a 'back door' or side entrance where defenders could slip out of the castle undetected and launch a counterattack (or make a quick escape).

Revetment — The facing of a bank/mound with timber, stone etc.

Ringwork — An earthwork castle consisting of an enclosure defended with a bank and ditch. Partial ringworks are built on promontories and only have defences on the more vulnerable side.

Shell-keep A stone wall enclosing the summit of a motte, usually with lean-to buildings ranged against the inner walls.

Spur A pyramidal buttress found on hexagonal or round towers which have square bases. The 'spur' is the corner angle which rises up the side of the tower.

Solar The name for the private chamber of the castle's lord. Usually located beyond the high table in the hall.

Tomen Welsh for a mound or motte.

Tumulus An antiquarian term for a Prehistoric burial mound.

Undercroft A vaulted chamber below a principal room.

Vault The arched stone roof of a tower, room etc. Some vaults have supporting ribs of masonry.

Wall-walk A pathway along the top of a wall or tower, behind the battlements.

REFERENCES

AC	*Archaeologia Cambrensis*
AJ	*Archaeological Journal*
Austin	D. Austin, Carew castle archaeological project (interim reports)
Avent	R. Avent, 'Sir Gar - studies in Carmarthenshire history' (1991)
AW	*Archaeology in Wales*
Brut	*Brut y Tywysogion* (Chronicles of the Princes) trans. T. Jones (University of Wales Press 1952).
CA	*The Carmarthenshire Antiquary*
CADW	*CADW: Welsh Historic Monuments.* Official guidebooks to castles in the care of CADW.
Ceredigion	*Ceredigion: Journal of the Cardiganshire Antiquary Society.*
Charles	B.G. Charles, 'Place-names of Pembrokeshire' (National Library of Wales 1992).
CS	*Carmarthenshire Studies* ed. T. Barnes, N. Yates (Carmarthen County Council 1974).
DAT	Dyfed Archaeological Trust, sites & monuments record.
Fort	*Fortress*, the castles and fortifications quarterly.
Fenton	Richard Fenton *Historical Tour through Pembrokeshire* c1811 (reprinted 1994 by Dyfed County Council).
Gerald	Gerald of Wales, *The Journey through Wales* in 1188 (available in several modern editions).
Griffiths	R. A. Griffiths, *Conquerors and Conquered in Medieval Wales* (Alan Sutton 1996).
H Owen	*Old Pembrokeshire Families*, Henry Owen (London 1902)
HKW	*History of the King's Works*, ed. H. M. Colvin (HMSO 1963).
HWC	*Houses of the Welsh Countryside* P. Smith (HMSO 1988).
Jones	Major Francis Jones, *Historic Houses of Pembrokeshire* (Brawdy Books 1996).
Jones 1977	I. G. Jones, 'Aberystwyth 1277-1977' (Gwasg Gomer 1977).
JPHS	*Journal of the Pembrokeshire Historical Society.*
King	D. J. C. King, *Castellarium Anglicanum* (Kraus International 1983).
Leland	*The Itinerary of John Leland* c1546.
Meyrick	Samuel Meyrick, *History and Antiquities of the County of Cardigan*, (1809).
Miles	D. Miles *Castles of Pembrokeshire* (Pembrokeshire Coast National Park Authority 1979).
MWL	Museum of Welsh Life, St Fagans (records of)
NMR	National Monuments Record for Wales (RCAHM)
Owen	George Owen of Henllys, 'Description of Penbrookshire' c1603. Available as *The Description of Pembrokeshire* Gomer Press (The Welsh Classics 1994)
RCAHM	Royal Commission on Ancient and Historical Monuments, Inventories of Carmarthenshire (1917), Pembrokeshire (1925), Newport Castle, an architectural study (1992)
Soulsby	I. Soulsby, *The Towns of Medieval Wales* (Phillimore 1983)

General reference sources.

Castles in Wales & the Marches – essays in honour of D. J. C. King ed. R. Avent & J. Kenyon (University of Wales Press 1987)

A History of Wales J. Davies (Penguin Press 1987)

Conquest, Coexistence and Change, 1063-1415 R. R. Davies (Clarendon Press/University of Wales Press 1987)

The Medieval castle in England and Wales – a social & political history N. J. G. Pounds (Cambridge University Press 1990)

The Rise of the Castle' & 'The Decline of the Castle M. W. Thompson (Cambridge University Press 1991 & 1988)